······ **THE** ······

FAUX PAS

SURVIVAL GUIDE

■■■■■■■■■■■■■■■■

ALSO BY JEANNE MARTINET

The Art of Mingling

Getting Beyond Hello: Miss Mingle's Guide to Navigating the Nineties

JEANNE MARTINET

▪▪▪▪▪▪ THE ▪▪▪▪▪▪

FAUX PAS

SURVIVAL GUIDE

THE FINE ART OF
REMOVING YOUR FOOT
FROM YOUR MOUTH

▪▪▪▪▪▪▪▪▪▪▪▪▪▪▪▪▪

ST. MARTIN'S GRIFFIN ❦ NEW YORK

Design by Pei Koay

Library of Congress Cataloging-in-Publication Data

Martinet, Jeanne.
    The faux pas survival guide : the fine art of removing your foot from your mouth / Jeanne Martinet.—1st St. Martin's Griffin ed.
       p.   cm.
    ISBN 0-312-14621-3
    1. Faux pas.   I. Title.
BJ1838.M37   1996
395'.3—dc20   96-19728
                                        CIP

First St. Martin's Griffin Edition: October 1996

10 9 8 7 6 5 4 3 2 1

CONTENTS

ACKNOWLEDGMENTS

I WOULD BE SURE to commit a faux pas should I attempt to name everyone who shared their personal faux pas horror stories—I would inevitably leave someone out, or list someone who would rather remain anonymous. I hope, therefore, that those who contributed to this book will accept my nonspecific but heartfelt gratitude.

I do need to offer special thanks to Carter Inskeep, Jason Harootunian, and my editors, Barbara Anderson and Marian Lizzi.

THE

FAUX PAS

SURVIVAL GUIDE

INTRODUCTION:
IS THAT A FOOT IN YOUR
MOUTH OR ARE YOU
JUST GLAD TO SEE ME?

YOU NEVER KNOW when it's going to happen.

You're having dinner with your friend Lisa and her friend Jill, whom you have never met before that evening. Everyone is getting along fine, and by the time you get to dessert, the conversation has turned to your favorite topic: finding a mate for you. Lisa begins describing her current candidate, a lawyer named Walter. She ends by saying, "Anyway, I think he sounds really good for you, don't you?"

"Oh, I don't know," you say, thinking with distaste about the last lawyer you dated.

"Well," Lisa admits, "maybe he would be a better match for Jill."

You look up from your chocolate torte with a lost look on your face. "Jill? Who's Jill?" you demand. There is a long moment of utter silence during which Lisa doesn't dare look at Jill;

she just puts down her spoon and buries her face in her hands. Light finally dawning, you blush a deep shade of magenta. You are horrified, but try to make a joke of it. "Wow—Jill—" you laugh, "I can't believe I just had a whole dinner with you and forgot your name!"

"Don't worry," Jill says to you, smiling sweetly. "I promise to forget yours later."

■　■　■

There are two terrifying things every human being must face. One of them is death. The other is the making of faux pas. Within the realm of social interaction, few things are more painful than that embarrassing, superconspicuous moment after you have just committed a really bad faux pas. Whether you've just called your hostess's new husband by the name of his predecessor or you've unwittingly divulged information about someone's adulterous sexual liaison, the backlash from a faux pas can knock you off your feet, psychologically, and really ruin your day.

While many people consider me to be an Expert Mingler, what they may not realize is that I also happen to be the Queen of Faux Pas. Making them, that is. I can put my foot in my mouth quicker and more fully than almost anyone I know. Just as an expert skier is more apt to break his leg, as an outgoing conversationalist I am more likely to make mistakes than a shier person. And because I *do* gravitate toward the "expert only" slopes, communication-wise, I am continually making faux pas: little ones, big ones, quiet ones, and noisy ones. I've made some astoundingly bad social gaffes, in fact, that made me and everyone around me want to vanish like last night's bad dream. But one benefit of my continual conversational bumbling is that over the years I have learned foolproof ways (from trial and error—and I do mean *error!*) to smooth over or recover from just about every possible social blunder, snafu, slip of the tongue, or lapse. Mistakes, after all, are the best teachers. If you've never made a mess, you can't know the best way to clean it up.

Now, there are harmless faux pas that make you and everyone around you laugh; and then there are the type that make you feel like screaming in agony. I seem to lean toward the more embarrassing kind, and usually commit them with an extra-humiliating amount of drama and noise. I don't have to be at a social event, either. The scary thing about faux pas is that they happen when you least expect them—anywhere, anytime. Just when you think you're safe from all potential social booby traps (when you're going out to mail a letter, for example, and you happen to step on someone's foot and say, "Excuse me, sir," before looking up into a distinctly female face), you find yourself zapped by one that has snuck up from behind.

One particularly memorable and complex conversational catastrophe I caused took place right outside my front door. I had been up all night trying to meet a deadline and was a wreck—dirty hair, bloodshot eyes, rumpled clothing— definitely in no shape for socializing. I was just going out for a quick bite, but as I opened my apartment door I ran smack into what I surmised were my new next-door neighbors, whom I had not yet met. They were a man and a woman, with two large dogs and a baby in tow.

Considering the state I was in, I probably should have said, "Excuse me, I forgot my wallet," and gone right back inside. Instead, I plunged headlong into conversation while we waited for the elevator.

"Hi! Welcome! I see you have two dogs . . . I have a cat . . . You should know that you're not meeting the real me right now. I've been up all night—literally all night, I mean it—on deadline; I'm a writer, you know, no, well, I guess you wouldn't know—and anyway, I haven't slept at all . . ." I was aware, even through my haze, that this was not a good start. I was not making a good impression. But I could not seem to stop talking. The whole family was staring blankly at me (even the dogs). The elevator came. We squeezed in, stroller and all.

It was now time for me to recoup, to try to correct the bad first impression I was making. I smiled down at their baby, resorting to what I knew to be the one and only surefire method of winning over parents. "Oh, what an incredibly beautiful little girl!" Oops. I knew immediately the chances were fifty-fifty that I had just committed one of the world's most common faux pas. Sure enough:

"It's a boy," the woman said stiffly. (It always amazes me how huffy people get when someone mistakes the sex of their tiny bald baby.)

"Oh, of course, how cute!" I responded, trying desperately to regain my footing. I peered down at the infant as though looking at it for the first time, and noticed it had a large, nasty-looking scab on its forehead.

"Ohhh," I cooed disgustingly, "and what happwened to the wittle one's sweet wittle he-ead?" I couldn't believe this was me talking in baby talk. Had some evil spirit taken over my body? Then I saw that my neighbors had funny expressions on their faces, and something told me they weren't merely reacting to the baby talk. Uh-oh, I thought, maybe they hit their child on the head or something and I shouldn't have asked about the scab.

"It's a birthmark," the man said in a quiet voice.

Ouch. This was really awful. But still I kept going, like a runaway train.

"Well, he could always grow up and take over Russia!" I said gaily. There was a terrible silence, during which the couple glanced at each other. Then the woman gave me a slight smile.

"I suppose so," she said.

Luckily, the doors opened before I could do further damage, which was a very good thing because in a minute I would probably have managed to insult the dogs. I flew out of that elevator as if it were on fire. (P.S.: I did manage to redeem myself with my neighbors later on, using an "After-the-Fact" faux pas recovery method [see page 65]. But it wasn't easy.)

Of course, faux pas that occur in elevators are your worst-case scenario, because there is often not enough time to undo the damage. Certainly most faux pas are not this dreadful (a multiple faux pas plus a flubbed recovery attempt), and most are much easier to repair. And, believe it or not, some social slipups can actually break the ice, or cause some unexpected, beneficial result. If you are well practiced, you might even turn a bad faux pas to your advantage. But no matter what kind of faux pas you commit, there is one thing you must realize: *Everyone makes them.* It's built into our DNA! While some people have more of a tendency to commit faux pas than others (it's a metabolism thing), no one can avoid all faux pas unless he stays at home with the shades drawn and doesn't answer the phone.

In researching this book I have collected hundreds of stories about faux pas—faux pas committed on airplanes, in trains, in the office, by mail, in rest rooms, in restaurants, in the bedroom, on the street, at the gym, on the beach, at cocktail parties, in line for the movies, at dinner parties, at reunions, at baby showers, in the classroom, on answering machines, at weddings, in hospitals, at funerals, or while in the kitchen just sipping tea. No one, it seems, is immune, and no location safe. (In fact, after reading about some of these faux pas, you may decide that on a scale of one to ten, you are pretty darn smooth!)

We all *know* that to err is human; and yet most people who commit faux pas react like criminals caught in police floodlights. Many people actually close their eyes under the force of their mortification, not unlike children who think that if they can't see anyone, no one can see them. Some people find themselves literally praying that they could die on the spot. (Note: In spite of rumors to the contrary, you cannot actually die of embarrassment. I have heard of someone being sick for a couple days, but that was an extreme case.) Some faux pas perpetrators actually pinch themselves, hoping that they are merely having a nightmare from which they can awake. People who work a lot with computers will visualize pushing the "undo" key. After a really bad goof, I've sometimes had an insane impulse to fill the terrible post faux pas pause with a loud and piercing scream. Sometimes faux pas-ers can be so humiliated, it takes them days, even weeks, to get over it.

All this self-denigrating panic is totally unnecessary! By following simple guidelines and employing various easy-to-remember lines and techniques, you can avoid committing many faux pas, and learn to recover—more or less gracefully—from 99.99 percent of the ones you *do* commit. And since faux pas phobia is one of the biggest social inhibitors, once you no longer live in terror of committing faux pas, you may find your entire social life improving markedly. You will be confident that no matter what kind of chaos you create, no matter what sort of embarrassment ensues from an error, you will be able to weather the storm.

The Faux Pas Survival Guide will give you tips on knowing when you are likely to make a faux pas, and easy-to-follow rules to help you avoid it. It will also provide you with basic recovery techniques to get you through anything (faux pas–wise) that might happen to you, as well as offering you a wide array of field-tested faux pas recovery lines tailored to specific faux pas situations. My survival system—created from much research and painful personal experience—will prepare you to handle any faux pas, from a simple introduction mangle to a full-fledged relationship wrecker. You will even learn how to deal with dire disasters like compounded or multiple faux pas.

So fasten your seat belts, sit back, and get ready to face your faux pas fears—and banish them forever.

..... 1 .....

DEFINING

THE FAUX PAS

....

FAUX PAS (a noun, pronounced fō-'pä in the singular and fō-'päz in the plural): a slip or blunder in manners or conduct; a mistake in etiquette or propriety; a social blunder or indiscretion.

FAUX PAS OR NE FAUX PAS

Almost everybody will agree that faux pas are awkward, undesirable things to be avoided at all costs, that they frequently get in the way of having a good time, and that they can be a detriment to one's social success. But what exactly *is* a faux pas, and why are they so darned embarrassing? Why should we need advice on how to overcome them? How do we even know when we have made one?

I have met a few very lucky people who are virtually faux pas–proof—people who at least *seem* unaware of their own mistakes. Nothing embarrasses them, and if you try to point out their faux pas to them, they will only shrug or laugh. (These rare individuals are either highly evolved beings or in need of sensitivity training.) Most people, however, are all too mindful of their social foibles and either realize they have "faux pas-ed" the instant they've done it or are conscious that *something* bad has happened—even if they are not quite sure what. Some people have a delayed reaction to faux pas; in fact, I've been known to commit one and chatter on in a totally oblivious fashion for several minutes, like a driver who has run over a nail and doesn't realize it until all the air has leaked out of her tire. If you are someone who has trouble knowing right away when you have made a faux pas, here are some external clues to help you. You are more than likely facing a faux pas situation if:

- People around you suddenly stop talking.
- People around you begin moving away for no apparent reason.
- Your face gets hot, your heart stops beating, or you find you can't breathe. (Warning: Strong physical attraction causes similar symptoms.)
- The person to whom you are talking looks disturbed.
- The person to whom you are talking begins to cry.
- The person to whom you are talking slaps or punches you.
- The last words out of your mouth seem to echo loudly in the room or hang over your head like a helium balloon.
- You suddenly have an intense longing for your mother.

Faux pas make us feel horrible because, whether or not we've just called someone by the wrong name or pushed someone into the punch bowl, we have somehow broken an unwritten social code. This subtle (and ever-shifting) code of manners and public behavior is designed to help protect us from hurting each other; it's what makes it possible for us to live fairly comfortably together. Until we've broken one, and experienced the ensuing confusion, humiliation, and/or remorse, it's difficult to comprehend the importance of these seemingly trivial rules.

The subject of making faux pas is such a sensitive area for people that many are completely unable to remember most of the faux pas they've made. This is due, in part, to the fact that human memories are efficient machines, constructed to help us survive emotionally. We tend to block out the unpleasant things in our past, like the pain of childbirth, or like the time a young woman I know called her boyfriend to talk about sex and realized after ten minutes that it was not her friend but his father on the line. (If you ask her about it today, she's hazy about the entire incident.) In fact, it's quite revealing that we have no appropriate English word for these types of blunders, and that we instead use the fluffy, light-sounding French phrase *faux pas* (which translated literally means "false step") to soften the horror of the occurrence.

As bad as a faux pas can make you feel, it is a relatively small transgression, as human transgressions go. Although a faux pas is more than just a simple mistake, it is certainly less than a crime. Somewhere between forgetting your umbrella when it's raining and stealing someone's purse lies the vast, murky territory of faux pas. Before we can attempt to learn how to avoid or recover from faux pas, we need to be able to recognize them. (You don't want to waste apologies or other survival methods on non–faux pas). To qualify as an actual, honest-to-goodness faux pas, your deed or utterance must meet the following criteria:

1. It is a mistake you could have avoided.

2. It involves at least one other person (even if that person is just a spectator).

3. It usually makes you feel embarrassed if not downright horrible.

4. It often makes someone else feel embarrassed if not downright horrible.

There are, of course, embarrassing moments that are *not* faux pas, like when someone convinces you at a party to do your Jerry Lewis impersonation and nobody laughs, or when you find out your mother-in-law has read your diary. If you'd like to measure your faux pas savvy, take this quick faux pas quiz. Which of the following situations would you consider to be a faux pas and which would you not?

QUICK FAUX PAS QUIZ

1. You run into an old friend in the grocery store and inquire about her husband. The friend looks pained and pauses before replying softly, "Well . . . he's . . . he died." (Faux pas, or ne faux pas?)

Answer: This, while admittedly an awful moment, is not a faux pas, for the simple reason that you could not have known that the husband had died. Express your condolences, but never feel embarrassed for something you had no way of avoiding.

2. You are at an art gallery opening; your escort is a close friend of the artist whose work is being shown. After mingling with various groups of people, you return to talk to a woman with whom you have chatted previously but to whom you have not been formally introduced. During a pause in the conversation, you say to her, "So, are you an artist, too?" She responds somewhat coolly, "Actually, this is *my* opening." (Faux pas, or ne faux pas?)

Answer: This one *is* a faux pas. Because your escort is a close friend of the featured artist, you should have made an effort to identify her and be introduced. Your escort, who should have made it his job to introduce you to his friend, must bear some of the blame.

3. You attend a reading given by a famous writer whose class you took three years ago when you were in college. After the reading you walk up and address the writer by her first name with a jovial "Hey, ———! Good to see you!" (Faux pas, or ne faux pas?)

Answer: This amount of familiarity, given the situation, is inappropriate; your salutation therefore constitutes a faux pas. Assuming a relationship that does not exist will not endear you to the person, and usually has the opposite effect. It is far better to err in the opposite direction and be too formal with someone than to cross the boundary in this manner.

4. You hear someone talking about a children's book you've heard of and you make the comment "Oh, that story is so heartwarming!" It's only after you see the bewildered looks on people's faces that you suspect something is wrong. It turns out they weren't discussing a children's book at all but a movie about Vietnam—with a similar title. (Faux pas, or ne faux pas?)

Answer: This is a faux pas *only* if the reason for the misunderstanding was your inattention (in other words, if, given the nature of the conversation, you should have known they were talking about a movie) and not an "honest" mistake (that is, that the two titles *are* extremely similar and the way the conversation unfolded up to a point did nothing to disabuse you of the conviction they were talking about a book).

5. You and a friend are listening to an audiotape made by his band when he was in college several years ago. He's told you he played bass in the band and he's asked you for your honest opinion. While you like the music—and tell him so— you feel compelled to express your dislike of the lead singer (who you remark sounds too "whiny"), never suspecting that the singer is none other than the friend. (Faux pas, or ne faux pas?)

Answer: Here you have fallen into the number one faux pas trap—that of erroneous assumption. You wrongly assumed that because your friend played bass, he could not also be the lead singer. (You also assumed he really wanted your honest opinion, which no performer ever does unless it's a positive one). This is a faux pas that could easily have been avoided by asking a few questions before venturing an opinion.

6. You meet an acquaintance at a dinner party. He is dressed uncharacteristically in an Armani suit. To flatter him, you make this enthusiastic observation: "God, you look so great! Really, I've never seen you dressed so well!" (Faux pas, or ne faux pas?)

Answer: Faux Pas. This is what is commonly referred to as a backhanded compliment. In other words, what was intended as praise has come forth as an insult. The Armani-clad man is now painfully aware that you have found him poorly dressed on most other occasions.

7. You are in an elevator, passionately kissing your mate. Without your realizing it, the elevator doors have opened to a crowd of awaiting passengers while you are still conspicuously entwined. (Faux pas, or ne faux pas?)

Answer: At the risk of sounding like a prude, in my book this is most certainly a faux pas, although it probably wouldn't be considered one in many cultures. Public displays of passion (I don't mean casual or quick kisses) are an intrusion not only on people's psychological space, but also on their physical space. An elevator is a small place that other people are going to have to enter. No one should be expected to have to get into a five-by-five-foot cubicle with a seriously smooching couple.

8. You are on a coffee break at a business conference. The room is crowded, and someone knocks into you right after you have poured yourself some hot coffee. The steaming brew slops out of your cup, landing painfully all over the front of the crisp white blouse of your boss. (Faux pas, or ne faux pas?)

Answer: This may feel like a faux pas, and in fact, it could make for a very unpleasant few moments. The accident was not your fault, however, and fault is one of the hallmarks of an actual faux pas. Your attitude should be similar to what it would be if both of you had been hit by a car, but you were not hurt while your boss was. The appropriate response is to express your sympathy, offer to help with any stain removal procedures, and explain that someone pushed you.

9. You are mailing a party invitation to a group of friends who happen to share a house. You can't remember all their names in full, so you address the invitation to the one you know best and assume she will inform her housemates. (Faux pas, or ne faux pas?)

Answer: This is a good example of a faux pas by mail. You belittle the other people by not including them on the invitation. Go to the small trouble of privately asking your good friend to give you the names of the housemates. And do make sure you spell the names correctly.

10. You are asked out by someone you don't particularly like. You don't want to hurt his feelings, so you tell him you can't go out with him because you are not feeling well. Later that night, you run into him at the movies, where you decided to go on the spur of the moment with a friend. (Faux pas, or ne faux pas?)

Answer: This is an extremely bad faux pas because you have been caught in a lie *and* have hurt someone's feelings terribly. It would have been better to tell the man you already had plans. Never use an illness excuse unless you are willing to act the part.

A WORD ABOUT ETIQUETTE

While I was interviewing people for this book, one overzealous contributor said to me, "I know a faux pas you should discuss. What about those absolutely horrid people who, when eating chocolates, leave the paper wrappers behind in the box?" Though it might well be considered a grievous faux pas in some circles, this is the kind of breach of etiquette that you either avoid or you don't, depending on what you have been taught and how much you care about having sophisticated manners. It is not, however, the kind of thing that is substantial enough to make too much fuss about. Let's be honest; the memory of those empty wrappers is not going to keep you up nights.

This is not to say that manners are not important. Rules of behavior are essential for the smooth flow of civilized society, and are a great solace to most people. They help us fight our fear of chaos. But it is not the purpose of this book to delve into complicated matters of table manners, attire, or address. For one thing, many rules of etiquette—which were invented for the comfort and well-being of society, not its imprisonment— are changing to accommodate modern lifestyles. (Very few people today can be expected to have four different kinds of sterling silver forks to set at lunch, for instance). Also, there are already many useful reference books on these subjects, by many thorough and well-intentioned experts, including Amy Vanderbilt, Mrs. Humphry, Alice Leone Moats, Emily Post, Letitia Baldridge, and Marjabelle Young Stewart, to name a few.

Most people will agree, I think, that in today's frightening quagmire of social interaction there are much scarier and more difficult problems to handle—moments when you have hit a serious and noticeable snag, when you have definitely crossed over the line of acceptable behavior and you (and others) know without a doubt that you should never have done or said a particular thing. You know it instinctively, immediately. You are standing there with panic in your brain and guilt in your soul. Real faux pas are not, for the most part, about form; they are about substance. In other words, we are not talking about cases of trivial awkwardness such as not using your finger bowl properly. (Although, if you were to *drink* from your finger bowl because you think it's clear soup, *that* would be a faux pas.) Whether or not something constitutes a faux pas has much to do with your own level of embarrassment. To a great extent, it is subjective; you and any witnesses decide in a flash whether or not a faux pas has been committed.

An authentic faux pas is something unexpected and awful, something that cries out for recovery tactics. You do not need the faux pas recovery techniques and lines in this book for forgetting to say "Thank you." You do need them if you *mean* to say thank you but for some reason it comes out of your mouth "Spank you."

FAUX PAS-IBILITIES: THE FIVE FAUX PAS CATEGORIES

There are many different settings and circumstances for committing faux pas, but there are only five major categories of faux pas you can commit. Don't worry, all are survivable.

1. Getting Caught. This kind of faux pas includes those occasions when you are discovered to be lying about something or someone; when you are overheard saying something you know you shouldn't; when you are caught telling secrets that you swore not to reveal; or when you get caught pretending to know something or somebody you don't. This variety of faux pas usually carries a high embarrassment factor.

2. Being Mean. Insulting someone *without meaning to* is a classic faux pas situation. (Note: If you do it on purpose, it drops out of the domain of faux pas and into that of abuse.) This encompasses careless comments as well as compliments that go awry, and is the type of faux pas most often referred to as "foot-in-mouth" disease.

3. Behaving in an Inappropriate Manner. If you ask embarrassing questions or make inappropriate observations—or use profanity or bring up vulgar subjects—you are committing this kind of faux pas. Inappropriate actions (overly familiar ones, for example) also qualify as category-three faux pas. This category covers most "physical" faux pas—instances of lewdness, clumsiness, sloppiness, or drunkenness.

4. Faux Pas of Omission. This is the kind of social error in which you are guilty of an actual lapse, for example, if you obviously failed to introduce someone, or if you invited everyone but one person in a group to a party.

5. Saying or Doing Something That's Just Plain Dumb. This describes the kind of faux pas that involves revealing yourself to be ignorant of something about which you should not be ignorant. It is about having a lack of knowledge *when you really should know better.* This covers incidents such as calling someone by the wrong name or misunderstanding something essential to a conversation. It also includes those bizarre times when your mouth just doesn't work quite right and you end up saying things you didn't plan to say.

CROSS-CULTURAL CONFUSIONS

A few years ago, a physician friend of mine got a job practicing medicine in Samoa. (To protect his professional reputation I'll call him "Dr. C.") On his very first day at work a man came to the hospital complaining of severe stomach pains. Dr. C., in an effort to be cross-culturally sensitive in his new environment, had tried to learn as much as he could about Samoan culture. He had read that many Samoans visited faith healers and that the word for faith healer in Samoan was *fau-fau*. While examining his patient, Dr. C. asked the man if he had tried the *fau-fau* (which he pronounced *foo-foo*) before he had come to the hospital. Much to Dr. C.'s surprise, the man turned bright red, cast his eyes to the floor, and shook his head. Just then a nurse who had happened to overhear leaned over to Dr. C. and said with a slight smile, "Doctor, the word for healer is pronounced *fo-fo*, not *foo-foo*. *Foo-foo* means to masturbate."

This kind of blunder is always extremely disconcerting (I think Dr. C. turned redder than his patient); however, errors that stem from differences in culture or language are entirely excusable and are therefore exempt from all the rules and recovery systems that pertain to faux pas. Cross-cultural confusions are, in large part, simply unavoidable, whether they be language mistakes or mistakes of gesture or action. The cases of this type of intranational misunderstanding are so numerous, one could fill a book with them—from eating with your left hand in Saudi Arabia, to giving someone an A-OK signal (making a circle with your thumb and index finger) in Mexico, to exposing the soles of your feet in India. And though these mix-ups may be painful, some eventually lead to greater sympathy between cultures, once the confusion has been cleared up.

The only way you can lessen the possibility of these foreign flubs is to immerse yourself in the language or culture to which you are going to be exposed, and then to stay alert and tread very carefully. If you are in a foreign country, your ability to tell when you have made such a mistake may be impaired. You'll need to watch closely for evidence that you have insulted or embarrassed someone (or yourself). It's also not a bad idea to have an apologetic phrase at the ready in the language in question, something to the effect of "I haven't been in your country very long" or "So sorry, I am only an ignorant tourist."

FAUX PAS PHOBIA AND WHAT IT CAN DO TO YOUR SOCIAL HEALTH

In my previous book, *The Art of Mingling*, I identified a widespread social disease known as *minglephobia*, which is a fear of talking to strangers. There exists a related disorder that is just as crippling as minglephobia and that affects just as many people: *faux pas phobia.*

Like minglephobia, faux pas phobia greatly hinders our social ease and success, our spiritual well-being, and (most important) our having a good time. Most people's social inhibitions stem from this deep-seated "error terror"—a fear of messing up in some way, of appearing inept, of looking stupid, of showing other people our failings, or of hurting someone's feelings. The social skittishness that results from faux pas phobia can seriously affect your life. Unless you deal head-on with your faux pas phobia, it will constrict and restrict your social ability to such an extent that you may become timid, reserved, repressed—or (even more horrifying) boring.

How do we contract faux pas phobia in the first place? Simple: from our memories of past faux pas, whether committed by us or merely witnessed. Consciously or subconsciously, we remember the emotional pain—the shame, the feelings of inadequacy—that accompanied former faux pas. These faux pas memories are part of the psychological baggage we carry with us into every social setting. Our anxiety about committing faux pas is based on the firsthand experience of knowing what it feels like.

I know someone so traumatized by a childhood faux pas (she was saying something extremely mean about an unpopular girl in her class and was overheard by her) that she believes it affects her social behavior to this day. When she is in public and is talking about anyone not present, even if the subject matter is not even remotely negative in nature, she drops her voice to barely above a whisper until her listeners beg her to speak up. She is absolutely petrified of being overheard.

Many people are handicapped to one degree or another by faux pas phobia. I have received letters from people who confess that out of fear of giving offense, they will often avoid conversational topics that are of interest to them, if those areas seem even the slightest bit too personal, too sensitive, or problematic. Alas: the greatest tragedy of faux pas phobia is that living in perpetual fear of making a mistake often cuts you off from the juiciest part of the conversational "fruit" each person you encounter has to offer.

This is why learning to recover from faux pas is so essential to your social health. Face it: you *are* going to make *some* faux pas, unless you never go out and never answer the phone. But once equipped with your personal "faux pas recovery kit," your backup bag of tricks, you will begin to feel freer, socially speaking, than ever before. If you know you've got the cure, you won't be so afraid of the affliction. Instead of being paralyzed by your fear of slipping up, you will be energized by the confidence that you can recover from any faux pas fall.

.... 2 ....

HOW TO
AVOID
FAUX PAS

WHILE IT'S TRUE that you shouldn't let the fear of making faux pas rule your social life, there are plenty of faux pas that can easily be avoided—without impinging on your social style. All you need to do is follow a few basic safety rules, learn to be wary when you are swimming in dangerous waters, and steer clear of the most common pitfalls.

WARNING SIGNS: RECOGNIZING FAUX PAS DANGER ZONES

I have made so many faux pas in my life that I have a fairly good early detection system; that is, I know on what occasions I am likely to mess up. (Unfortunately, all too often I ignore the alarm bells.) I have even been known to turn to the person next to me and say, "I can tell I am going to make a lot of faux pas tonight." This foreknowledge might rattle some people; but because I have myriad faux pas recovery techniques at the ready,

I no longer suffer from any but the mildest case of faux pas phobia, and therefore am usually only slightly concerned about the probability of my "faux pas-ing."

My faux pas warning system is connected not to my surroundings, but to my emotional or psychological state. It is a proven fact that most faux pas occur when we are nervous, tired, stressed out, tipsy, distracted, daydreaming, excited, aroused, rushed, or otherwise overtaxed or out-of-focus. (These states describe nearly every waking moment for me!) It is at these times that your tongue refuses to obey, that your feet don't work properly, and that your mind goes out of gear. The unfortunate truth is that faux pas are usually made during those moments when making one is much worse than it would be at another time, like when you are on a blind date or an important job interview, or are meeting your in-laws for the first time.

Learning to avoid faux pas means learning to be more careful when you are in these highly vulnerable states. Just as most people would have to be cautious while walking in six-inch spiked heels, so should you proceed with care in social situations when you know you are not feeling totally "up to snuff." You can still take part in every encounter or activity you like, just be sure to concentrate a little more than usual on what it is you are doing or saying. You may even want to avoid certain subjects altogether, depending upon how "off" you are feeling. Everyone's faux pas tendencies are different; some people make more after two drinks while some people make fewer. If you can begin to recognize your own ripe arenas for faux pas, you may ward off a great many social disasters.

But remember: Being careful doesn't mean being fearful. It just means becoming more knowledgeable about your personal faux pas climates. If it turns out you make faux pas only when you drink Scotch, you may want to consider switching to wine spritzers.

THE FOUR ANTI–FAUX PAS RULES

Before we tackle the problem of how to sidestep the most common faux pas, there are some important rules you need to try to incorporate into all of your interpersonal communications, whether they be in person, in writing, or on the phone. These rules may sound simplistic, but take my word for it, they will serve you well. In fact, many faux pas can be averted just by following these four anti–faux pas rules.

■ ■

1. Never assume.
(This is a good rule to follow in all things, not just when you're socializing.)

2. Think before you speak.
(Specifically, think about *who* it is you are talking—or writing—to in relation to *what* you are about to say.)

3. Always be aware of who is within earshot.
(But try not to scan the area around you in a conspicuous manner; you don't want to look paranoid.)

4. When in doubt, admit your ignorance.
(It's far better to admit you don't know what people are talking about than to *demonstrate* you don't know what people are talking about.)

■ ■

It may take a lot of practice before these rules become an automatic part of your interaction with others in the world, but the number of committed faux pas will be substantially reduced if you can remember them even half of the time. If you find it hard to think about these four tenets *and* carry on conversations, you might want to practice them one at a time (though they are by their nature interconnected); in other words, one night you might concentrate only on *not assuming*. At the next party, focus on another rule. You may be surprised how quickly your social psyche is affected.

THE WORLD'S MOST COMMON FAUX PAS AND HOW TO NEVER MAKE THEM AGAIN

While adhering to the four rules can help you avoid many faux pas, there are several commonly committed faux pas it helps to watch out for. Each of us has committed each of these social slips at least once in our lives; and for mistakes of this magnitude, once is certainly enough. If we can be on the lookout for these typical faux pas, we can avoid many of them.

Familial Assumptions: Getting it Wrong

Picture this: You arrive at a party. You see a man you recognize standing with someone you do not—a young woman who is no more than half his age. You go up to the two of them and, addressing yourself to the woman, you say, "So, you must be [name of man]'s daughter." Inevitably, she turns out to be (as she informs you rather frostily) not his daughter, but his wife.

There are many versions of this classic faux pas. For example, recently a friend of mine was being shown some family photos by a female colleague. After looking at one of the pictures, my friend pointed to a person in the photo and said to the colleague, "Oh, is this your son?" to which the colleague replied, "No it's my brother." (This comment, of course, implied that the woman looked old enough to be the person's mother).

On another occasion one of my aunts—who prides herself on being circumspect in her manners—attended a buffet supper party at the home of Dr. H., a school principal as well as her boss. At the proper time she approached Dr. H. and his wife, who was cutting the cake beside him.

"Everything is delicious, Mrs. H.," my aunt said. "Thank you so much for inviting me."

"I'm glad you could come," the woman replied, "but I'm not Mrs. H. I'm her sister-in-law." What was embarrassing to my aunt was that she had met Mrs. H. once or twice before, and Dr. H.—who was within earshot—knew it.

Another friend, David, made one of the most extreme forms of Familial Assumption while attending his tenth college reunion. (Reunions are, by the way, faux pas minefields. Everything is so familiar and yet so different.) He was standing around chatting with friends. One of his old fraternity brothers, Donny, introduced him to his wife. David said, "Oh, we met at the fifth reunion." His other friends stirred slightly.

"No, I don't think so," said Donny.

"Yes, I'm sure I did," David kept insisting, cheerfully oblivious to the increasing tension around him.

"No, you didn't," Donny said evenly. "That was my first wife." (According to David, the best response he could come up with after this news was "Ah.")

Whether you've mistaken someone's gay lover for his father, or someone's maid for her daughter, this kind of blunder can be paralyzing. Almost everyone is guilty of having committed this social sin at one time or another, and yet it is one of the easiest mistakes to avoid if we would only adhere to the number one rule in avoiding faux pas: *Never assume.*

More than half of all the faux pas in the social universe occur because someone makes an erroneous assumption about something. The urge to assume is born of our natural desire to be right, to appear smart, to be "in the know." Most people hate to be wrong; their egos make them *expect* that they will know things about other people or about their surroundings. Assuming makes us feel comforted, in control.

Never be afraid to admit you need information! (See Anti–Faux Pas Rule Number Four, on page 26.) It's important and realistic to ask questions when you're out in the world. Practice this exercise: Before you open your mouth to say something, think, "Am I about to make a *statement* about this person's relationship with someone?" If you are, you'd better be absolutely *positive* about the substance of that statement, or you should transform it into a *nonassumptive* question or statement, such as "So—how do you know Joe?" or "Have I met this lovely lady?" In fact, I highly recommend that you forever banish the dangerous lead-in phrase "You must be . . ." from your mingling vocabulary.

Under certain circumstances you may want to consider a truly elegant (if somewhat excessive) alternative to avoiding this brand of faux pas, and do what the Japanese do. As a culture, the Japanese are so intensely faux pas phobic that they will do anything to ensure that the familial-assumption faux pas (or any faux pas, for that matter) can't happen. I was reminded of this upon hearing a marvelous story about a certain Mr. Smith, who used to travel in Japan during the 1950s with his wife and his mother. When he would arrive at a hotel with the two "Mrs. Smiths," the clerk would almost always inquire politely, "Mr. Smith, which room will your *daughter* be taking?" This is a brilliant subterfuge: By purposely making a mistake one generation *down*, the clerk was not merely assured of not giving offense but effectively complimented everyone involved.

One last note: It doesn't hurt to do a little private reconnoitering before approaching someone you feel you are expected to know, especially if you suspect you may have met the person before. If you learn about a person's associations before speaking with him, you can avoid the Familial Assumption faux pas and hide your ignorance at the same time. But make sure your source for snooping is a good one. Beware of practical jokers, who may think it amusing to convince you the hostess's mother-in-law is her interior decorator.

Fertile Ground: Pregnancy Faux Pas

I don't think I exaggerate when I say that there is one kind of faux pas so dreadful that its perpetrator immediately loses all sensation in his hands and feet, because so much blood is rushing to his face. I am referring, of course, to the stupendously horrible act of asking a nonexpectant woman about her pregnancy.

It is amazing to me, considering its destructive impact, how many people make this faux pas. Pregnancy faux pas are among the top two or three most frequently committed faux pas—or, if they are not, they are at least the most memorable. Almost everyone I interviewed cited this as being in their past repertoire. I have both done this deed and had it done to me, and the embarrassment level is enormously high on either side of the Fertile Ground faux pas fence. The cruelest element of the pregnancy assumption is that even if your mistake was based entirely on nonvisual criteria, your comment will without exception be taken as a negative observation about the person in question's weight. The way this nightmare usually plays out is this:

You walk up to someone who has a bulging stomach and/or is wearing something flowing or high-waisted, and you ask, "When are you due?" What follows—if indeed the woman is not anticipating a blessed event—is usually stunned silence. (I believe this is where the term *pregnant pause* came from.) Then the insulted victim will respond with one of a wide variety of denials, anything from a generous "Oh, it's this darned dress, people always think that" to a cold and crushing "I *beg* your pardon!" Often the woman is so mortified that she walks away without saying much of anything.

Listen up, folks. I am about to fix it so this never happens to you again. There is one absolute, hard-and-fast, no-exception rule that can save you from future bouts of this form of social suicide. It is really just a matter of remembering Anti–Faux Pas Rule Number One: Never assume. When talking to an apparently pregnant woman, *never, ever, ask about her pregnancy, until she or someone else brings it up first.* I'm not kidding when I say *never.* Better safe than sorry; it is *extremely* difficult to recover from this faux pas.

Naturally it's going to feel odd to omit this topic from your discourse if the woman is so large that her belly is protruding into your canapés; however, you can always say something like "So, how are you feeling?" which will lead gently into the subject but still leave you a way out. Even "You're certainly looking radiant!" is safe, because it doesn't *necessarily* refer to pregnancy. But never ask directly, "Are you pregnant?" or "Are congratulations in order?" In this case inquiry is no better than an out-and-out assumption; if the woman's answer is no, it conveys the same message: *You are so fat you look pregnant.*

If you can discipline yourself to obey this rule whenever you find yourself on Fertile Ground, you will never again have to face the fallout from this enormously embarrassing faux pas. It may be difficult to train yourself to resist commenting on something that seems so obvious, but believe me, self-control can be your salvation. This practice has become such second nature to me that it has saved me from certain disaster on numerous occasions. In fact, recently I ran into a woman who I had happened to hear through a friend was pregnant, and indeed she looked it; but because of my habit of never saying anything, I automatically refrained from the tempting, almost obligatory, "When are you due?" question. Thank God I did, for as our conversation progressed it became apparent that she'd already *had* the baby several weeks before!

As horrible as it is, mistaking a nonexpectant woman for an

expectant one is not the only possible pregnancy faux pas. Here are some other related danger areas to be aware of and avoid:

Conception: For some strange reason, many people feel free to ask an expectant mother whether the baby was planned or whether it was a "surprise." (!) Needless to say (although, from the reports I get, I *do* need to say it) this is a definite no-no.

Gender: This is a relatively new form of pregnancy faux pas. Because it is now possible to find out the sex of an unborn child, whether it's going to be a boy or girl is one of the questions people ask. The trouble is, while some couples have no problem sharing this advance information with the world, to others it is an extremely personal matter—and may be a bone of contention between the two. It is not a major crime to ask this question, but it is usually better to refrain. If you must, inquire about whether they have picked out any names, and surmise the gender from their answer. (Under no circumstances, however, are you to comment negatively on their choice of name or to begin suggesting names of your own. Expectant parents are bombarded with suggestions, and it's really none of anyone else's business. They get enough of this sort of unwelcome advice from their families.)

Unsolicited tummy touching: The fact that we have fewer personal boundaries today than we used to has created some beneficial results, but this is not one of them. While it is certainly understandable that you might long to know what a fetus-filled abdomen feels like, putting your hand on someone's stomach without her express invitation is tantamount to grabbing her breast without warning, which I can only hope most people wouldn't do. Nevertheless, an astonishing number of women complain about distant relatives and casual acquaintances feeling free to grope their wombs. As a rule, only intimates should even ask permission for this fetal familiarity.

Fertile-ground rules for mom: I recently heard an outrageous story about a reverse form of the above faux pas: Reportedly, a pregnant woman suddenly grabbed her male co-worker's hand during a meeting and placed it unexpectedly on her stomach, presumably because she had felt her child within stirring. Her co-worker was confused and embarrassed.

I don't think too many women would need to be told that doing this to anyone but a mate or an intimate friend is unacceptable behavior. Also, please don't bring up gory details of your last ob-gyn exam in front of anyone but your closest friends and family (and even then, not at dinner, please), and resist all urges to pass around those delivery-room photos of your C-section, unless specifically requested. It may also be approaching "faux pas-dom" to discuss how hard or easy it was for you to get pregnant in front of someone who you suspect may be having fertility problems.

Loudmouth Syndrome: When You're Overheard

I will always remember (unfortunately) an agonizing experience I had when in my teens. I was hanging out in my older brother's extremely "cool" hippie-pad room, which was lit only by black lights and lava lamps. No matter what time of the day it was, there were always at least four guys lying around in the dimness with my brother, listening to Monty Python or Led Zeppelin. On this occasion I heard, out of the corner of my ear, somebody mention someone whom my brother's friends were always putting down. (To prevent my committing a current faux pas, I'll call the object of these put-downs "Ron.") In a pathetic effort to be "one of the guys," I launched into a mean-spirited, sarcastic tirade against Ron—about his bad jokes, his "stupid come-ons," etc. I was just getting around to his personal hygiene when I began to detect something strange in the air around me—a kind of unnatural stillness. A terrible suspicion suddenly gripped my insides . . . Oh no, it couldn't be, I thought . . . but yes, over in a shadowy corner, a familiar shape moved, and then spoke. "Thanks a lot, Jeanne," said Ron, who had been there all along, partially obscured from view by a black-lit pillow.

Beware of dark rooms, low-lit restaurants, public or office rest rooms, and crowded subway platforms. Keep your back to the wall; develop eyes in the back of your head; perfect your peripheral vision. Shine a light in the corners before you open your mouth, if you must—it will be worth it to avoid the horror of Loudmouth Syndrome.

These embarrassing category-one (getting-caught) faux pas occur not only when you are trashing someone (which you shouldn't do anyway) but also when you are just being careless, like when you are warning a friend not to bring up the hostess's husband because he walked out on her last night, and you turn around and the hostess is standing there with a daiquiri and a smile for you—both frozen.

There are lots of possible scenarios for Loudmouth Syndrome. Someone can accidentally overhear something he or she shouldn't simply because you are talking too loudly, or because the music stops abruptly and unexpectedly. Perhaps you are in a restaurant and are talking about a person whom you believe to be in another state, but who turns out to be at the next table. Maybe your friend Jane tells you something scandalous about her boss, J.B., and because you are not aware J.B. is present—never having met J.B.—you respond to this gossip in an indiscreet manner, causing J.B. to overhear. You might even be on the telephone and forget that it's possible the person you are talking about could pick up the extension in the next room.

One time my uncle Herman was leaving a crowded Broadway theater after what he thought was a particularly bad play. He turned to his wife and said, "What a lot of imbeciles the audience was!" only to discover that the woman behind him was not his wife but one of the aforementioned imbeciles. (I think she may have subsequently hit him with her purse.)

The point is: These things probably won't happen; they usually don't. But when they do, they are *very* tough to smooth over. It is for these instances that Anti–Faux Pas Rule Number Three is important: *Always be aware of who is within earshot.* Make absolutely certain that those who are within hearing distance are not related in some way to the person or events you are talking about. Remember that when you speak ill of anyone, you are always in dangerous territory. It is usually best in social situations to try not to be negative about other people, present or not. There are plenty of positive topics to choose from in any given social second, and you are just *begging* for faux pas whenever you make the choice to be insulting or vicious. (You may think you are being very witty when you tell someone you think Mr. Billings's toupee looks like a dead cat, but Mrs. Billings won't think so.)

However, if you insist on dishing the dirt, do it in the corner of the room so that no one can sneak up from behind. Or take the lucky recipient of your gossip into another room entirely. With a little cautiousness on your part, you can talk about strangers—as well as friends and acquaintances—to your heart's delight and get away scott-free.

My Mouth Runneth Over: Talking to the Wrong Person

Avoiding Loudmouth Syndrome is a relatively simple matter compared with learning to dodge another common class of faux pas: saying the wrong thing to the wrong person. By *wrong person* I mean someone who can be hurt, embarrassed, or angered by your comments, while another person would not be. Below are some examples of this form of faux pas:

The Impressionist's backfire: At a party, you use a fake, exaggerated accent in order to be funny and then find out that one person in the group you are talking to actually has that accent or comes from the country you are mocking.

Missed connections: You go to the principal of your son's school to complain about a fellow student, only to discover, during the conversation, that the troublemaker is the principal's grandson.

Accidental exclusion: You are chatting on the phone with a good friend and happen to mention a great party you went to or are planning to attend. As soon as the words are out of your mouth you realize that your friend may not have been invited and probably expected to have been.

Rumormongering: You are repeating a rumor about person X (whom you've never met) and it turns out that person X is none other than the person to whom you are repeating the rumor.

Secret telling: You reveal a secret that you weren't supposed to tell, in front of the person who told you.

Pet peeves: You are talking to your boss, or your mother-in-law (or any person in whose good graces you'd like to be), and you remark that you think anyone who eats Velveeta cheese is a brain-dead zombie, and, of course, he or she is a Velveeta devotee.

In endeavoring to avoid this type of "sticky wicket," it is helpful to remember Rule Number Two: *Think before you speak.* Okay, I know: This is easier said than done. If we always had time and ability to think before speaking, we'd never make any faux pas. However, many of these snafus can be avoided by thinking very specifically about the person to whom you are speaking—and what his or her connection might be to the words you're about to utter. If the answer to your inner query is "I'm not sure," then beware.

For example, if you aren't certain, why assume no one in a group of people will have an accent? Take the time to meet everyone before doing your funny-accent shtick. Similarly, don't take it for granted that everyone prefers real cheese to cheese food. (While it's always dangerous to assume, it's especially risky to assume everyone shares your likes and dislikes.) Also, before repeating any rumors, or saying anything negative or inappropriate about a specific person, try to find out if the person with whom you are sharing this has any relationship or prior experience with the object of your negative comments. Remember where you are and who your audience is.

Admittedly you can't be prepared for everything; you are not omniscient and you *are* going to slip up. To learn enough about everyone around you to guarantee total faux pas freedom would take more research than is practical in the real world of social interaction—which tends to unfold in an unexpected manner. And while I know of one couple who reads the obituaries religiously for just this kind of who-is-related-to-whom information, in my experience it's much easier to take a few minutes on the spot to check out your environment before venturing into certain high-risk areas. Like looking down at the sidewalk to see if you are going to step in a puddle, it's acceptable—even advisable—to scope things out before you speak. Use a test line comparable to one of the following:

"You aren't by any chance a close friend of Joe Smith's, are you?"

"Are you acquainted with Joe Smith?"

"You're not the one who painted these paintings, are you?"

"Can I assume you are not a big fan of Velveeta cheese?"

"So how do you fit into the picture?"

Sense and Insensitivity: Touching Touchy Subjects

I had just come from my periodontist's office, and was in a highly excited state (a ripe arena for a faux pas) due to my having received the wonderful news that my gums were much improved and I didn't need surgery. I was meeting my friend Karen at a bar, and when I got there I began to go on at great length about how happy I was that my teeth were not going to fall out, and that the spaces between my teeth were not going to get bigger and bigger until they were huge gaping holes that would make me look eighty years old. All of a sudden I noticed Karen had a tense, odd look on her face, and I remembered with a guilty shock that she had a less-than-perfect mouth herself, and that she suffered from all the periodontal horrors I was boasting about having escaped.

There are some subjects that should have warning labels on them in our minds, to help us avoid this kind of faux pas. Bad teeth to a person with gum disease, drinking to an alcoholic, weight problems to an obese person, bad skin to someone with acne, cancer to a cancer patient, your promotion to a person who's been fired—even virginity to an oversensitive virgin—are all subjects that can lead to social disaster, and bringing them up constitutes a major faux pas *if we are aware beforehand of the correlation between the subject and the person* (see also the box on page 41).

For instance, let's say you are talking to your favorite bartender down at Joe's. You are complaining about your horrific day, and you exclaim to him, "I swear to you I am going to murder my boss—really, somebody get me a gun—it will be justifiable homicide!" The bartender attempts a smile and then moves down to the other side of the bar. You remember too late that his wife was shot and killed last May.

What makes this a faux pas is that you should have known better; you should have had the *sense* to remember such an important fact about a person to whom you are speaking. The subsequent shameful feeling that envelops you comes from embarrassment at your *insensitivity*. If a stranger had made this comment, the bartender might or might not be affected; but in any case it would not have been a faux pas on the part of the stranger, merely an honest—albeit unfortunate—mistake.

To keep from committing the damaging Sense and Insensitivity faux pas, try to make Anti–Faux Pas Rule Number Two—think before you speak—a permanent part of your focus in any social situation. Always ask yourself whose ears are getting the benefit of your words. Make sure the verbal gems you are spewing are not going to end up hurting someone.

■ □ ■ ■ ■ ■

SAFETY FIRST
Questions and Comments to Avoid

"How many children do you have?"
(The person may be childless and/or have fertility problems.)

"I hate people who smoke, don't you?"
(There are still a few tobacco lovers out there.)

"So how was the funeral?"
(You never want to make someone cry.)

"I know I shouldn't ask [say] this, but . . ."
(Usually your instinct was right.)

"I hear your kid's got a learning problem."
(Parents don't necessarily want to discuss this in casual conversation.)

"I was sorry to hear about your miscarriage."
(Not unless she brings it up first.)

■ ■

NARROW ESCAPES

There is an old joke about a man who approaches a grocery-store employee and asks for half a head of lettuce. The employee goes to his supervisor and says, "You won't believe this, but some stupid idiot would like to buy half a head of lettuce . . ." As he is speaking, he becomes suddenly aware that the man has followed him and is right behind him. The employee quickly continues, "And this gentleman would like to buy the other half."

Sometimes you realize right in the middle of a sentence that you are about to commit a really bad faux pas. Not many people are able to switch lanes in midthought like the grocery store employee. However, it *is* sometimes possible, when you suddenly discover you are about to crash and burn, to step on the brakes, fast.

If you feel that you are about to land in faux pas hot water, *stop immediately*, no matter how abrupt it may seem. An interruption in the rhythm of your conversation is nothing compared to what may happen if you do *not* stop. This aborting technique is especially useful for those times you are on the phone and you are just about to faux-pas, because over the phone it is not as hard to fake an interruption.

Sometimes your interruption will be so abrupt and complete that it necessitates your leaving the person you are talking to immediately, and sometimes it will not. If you do *not* exit immediately (or hang up) upon delivering the line, an interruption should give you the space/time to alter your subject or think of a different ending to your disastrous beginning.

Here are some lines to help you smooth over your slamming on the conversational brakes and get the conversation going again—in another direction:

(FULL STOP) *". . . I can't believe who just walked in."* ("Who?" someone will probably ask. Ignore them.) *"Excuse me. Sorry."*

(FULL STOP) *". . . What was I just saying? I just blanked out. Too much coffee today, I guess."*

(FULL STOP) *". . . I . . . Oh! I'm sorry but I just remembered I was supposed to phone someone an hour ago."*

(FULL STOP) *". . . Sorry . . . Your eyes are so distracting, I'm afraid I've lost my train of thought."*

(FULL STOP) *". . . I'm sorry, my boss just came in and is motioning that she needs to talk to me. Could I call you back?"*

···· 3 ····

BASIC
RECOVERY
TECHNIQUES

■■■■■■■■■■

UNFORTUNATELY, the majority of faux pas are *not* avoidable. Usually you never even see them coming; suddenly you are just standing there with proverbial egg all over your face. So what now? Do you stammer and blush? Moan and run away? Never see or speak to the person again? You are free, of course, to do any of these things. But before you change your name and move to a new country, why not try to repair the damage? There are many effective and creative (some of them even fun) methods of recovering gracefully from almost any kind of social blunder. All you need to do is choose the method most appropriate to the circumstances and most appealing to you.

CONFESSION, APOLOGY, AND OTHER ACTS OF CONTRITION

Sometimes the easiest thing to do after making an embarrassing faux pas is simply own up to it and say you're sorry. Most people—unless you break their leg or their priceless Ming vase—will be inclined to accept a sincere expression of remorse. There are all kinds of apologies, however. You wouldn't use the same kind of "I'm sorry" after gently bumping into someone as you would after insulting his wife. While only you can judge what brand of "I'm sorry" is required for the particular situation, here are your options.

The Prestrike Apology

There may be times when you are not quite sure anyone has noticed that you've erred. Perhaps no one says anything, but there is suddenly a slightly odd feeling in the air. Of course, you could just pray that no one was paying attention, but I have found that often the wisest course of action is to go ahead and acknowledge the mistake—just in case.

A friend of mine once sent a letter to an important business acquaintance regarding an upcoming conference. After mailing the letter, my friend realized he had misspelled the acquaintance's name on the envelope. While it was probable that the business acquaintance never actually saw the envelope, my friend thought it would be best to mention it in the event he had; so the next time he saw the acquaintance he said, "You got my letter? Great. You know, I'm embarrassed to say that I think I may have spelled your name wrong. I hate when people do that to me. I'm usually very careful about these things."

I find this technique very comforting; there is a straightforwardness about it. It also comes in handy when you are not sure if what you have just done actually *qualifies* as a faux pas. For example, once during a Christmas party I was talking to several journalists and for some reason referred to one of the journalists' wives as "that old ball and chain." (Strange things happen to me around the holidays.) None of the group blinked an eye, but nevertheless I shook my head and said, "Did I really say that? Did I really say 'old ball and chain'? I don't know what is happening to me—somebody call a doctor! Or maybe an exorcist."

Moral: Confession is good for the soul and is also sometimes the best way to play it safe.

The Self-Effacing Apology

With a self-effacing apology you gain the sympathy of the faux pas-ee by showing him that the faux pas has made you suffer. For example, you might say: "I can't believe I did [said] that . . . You must hate me, and I don't blame you if you do. I am such an idiot." Or: "Oh, I am *so* clumsy [stupid/lame]." Most people will take pity on you and spend the next ten minutes trying to make *you* feel better. (Caution: A little self-effacement goes a long way. Don't go on and on about how horrible you are or people around you may start agreeing.)

The Sophisticated Apology

If you are involved in a social gaffe of a minor kind, such as stepping on someone's toe, dropping a spoon, or interrupting a conversation, you might try the more debonair Sophisticated Apology, otherwise known as the European method: *"Pardonnez-moi"* or *"Mi scusi!"* (Excuse me.) With the right amount of playfulness this response can be both gay and subtle. You can also use a British accent ("Tirribly sorry, ducks") for the Sophisti-cate, but the most subtle form of this type of apology is hardly an apology at all: "Oh dear—*quel faux pas.*" (What a faux pas.)

When you say you're sorry in a foreign language, it softens the remark and allows you to excuse yourself with some amount of dignity. This kind of apology indicates that you be-lieve you haven't done anything *really* bad, but at the same time acknowledges some small fault on your part. (Note: The So-phisticated Apology works best amongst the *unsophisticated.* If you are in an ethnically or culturally diversified room, it's not a good idea to use this particular type of apology.)

The Religious Apology

You may want to try invoking the Lord's name: "Oh God, I *am so sorry!*" It impresses people when you call out God's name. (That's why many people find cursing so satisfying.)

The Solicitous Apology or Offers of Penance

Some people like to offer to "make it up" to the person they have offended. This can range from asking if the person is all right to offering to give something to the offended party.

Examples:

"Oh dear, have I insulted [hurt/embarrassed] you? Can you ever forgive me?"

"Please tell me what I can do to make this right."

"Can I pay for that?" ["You must *let me pay for your dry cleaning."]*

"Here: let me get you another drink [piece of cake, etc.]."

"I feel terrible. How about I wash your car every Sunday for a month?"

"Okay, I want you to insult me. Badly. Then we'll be even."

The Nonverbal Apology

In this form of expression you use no words at all. For example: cover your hands with your face and groan. Or hug or kiss the faux pas-ed person. You might even grab on to him as if to say, "Save me from the horrible embarrassment of this moment!" If the situation warrants, clasp your hands together in a begging forgiveness posture. (In extreme cases, you can even kneel.) For the more jaunty, less obsequious Nonverbal Apology, you can make an ironic bow, as if your faux pas was so spectacular that it is receiving applause. The most extreme form of Nonverbal Apology is to mime shooting or strangling yourself. One accompanies this action with a gunshot sound, or a choking or gagging noise. (Collapsing on the floor is optional.)

EXQUISITE EXCUSES

Apologies may suffice some of the time, but there are many situations when an apology is *not* the best solution. Let's say, for example, that you have committed a category-five faux pas. In other words, you have just revealed yourself to be ignorant of something of which you feel you *shouldn't* have been ignorant. Perhaps you're at a political fund-raiser and have just let it be known that you haven't a clue who X is (X being a highly influential figure in your political party). People are staring at you in stunned disbelief and disdain. They look as if they are wondering who let you in, and you are beginning to wonder the same thing.

Obviously an apology here would be a serious mistake. You don't want to add insult to injury by saying, in effect, "I'm sorry I'm so stupid." A lot of faux pas, in fact, are better handled by offering an excuse rather than by merely apologizing. Saying to a woman, "I'm sorry that I called you a man," period, simply isn't going to cut it. Without adding a reason for your faulty perception, it sounds as if you are saying, "I'm sorry I said it out loud, but you *do* look like a man." When you add the excuse (e.g., "I'm terribly sorry, I don't have my contacts in") you go a long way toward taking the whole thing back and escaping unscathed.

In general, using an excuse is a stronger recovery than an apology alone. So what if you have to lie? (Why do you think they call it sociaLIzing?) If the excuse isn't believable, it can at least be entertaining—and therefore diverting. Here are some tried-and-true alibis for your faux pas first aid kit:

Pretend You Are Sick

As excuses go, this is a good one (and may even be true). Society has been using the "I'm sick" excuse for centuries. Whether it is from a plain old headache or the more trendy sinus infection, feigning illness can excuse you from many a mistake. A simple "I'm so sorry, I haven't been feeling well tonight" will work for a minor faux pas; more serious problems may require something like, "I should never have come out tonight with this migraine—I'm not myself at all." Or even: "That wasn't me talking, that was my herniated disk . . . Forgive me, I'm in so much pain, I don't know what I'm doing."

Warning: Be very careful not to use this defense too much, lest you find that your body starts to believe what you are saying. Plus you may get a reputation as a hypochondriac.

Pretend You Are Having a Really Bad Day

This is often an easy stance to adopt because the chances are good that you are already feeling pretty lousy from the faux pas you have just made. Now all you have to do is pick four or five other terrible things that could very well have happened to you—you were splashed by a taxi, were yelled at by your boss, were fired from a job, had your wallet stolen, were notified you're being audited, discovered the man you are dating is married—and recount the fictional horror story of your day. (There are some days you will have to exaggerate only a little bit!) Your freshly made faux pas will then become just another part of this "bad day," just a small piece of a run of bad luck, with which everyone can empathize.

Pretend You Took Too Many Painkillers

This excuse is similar to the illness excuse except that the illness excuse elicits sympathy, while this one, merely understanding. Almost everyone has, at one time or other, accidentally taken too many allergy pills, painkillers, cold tablets, etc., and found their emotional reactions impaired or their mood altered. But make sure people to whom you offer this excuse are clear that you are talking about medication, not recreational drugs. "Sorry, man, I'm tripping" is *not* an acceptable excuse in most social circles.

Pretend You Have Been in a Foreign Country Where the Customs Are Different

Because of the faux pas exemption that exists in cases of cross-cultural confusion, this can be a fun and adventurous justification for certain faux pas. Maybe you've just been seen tapping your ashes into the plate of discarded shrimp tails; or you are absentmindedly crushing ice in your mouth and a piece pops out, striking another person in the face before falling to the floor. Just smile, shake your head derisively, and say, "You must excuse me, I forget I'm not in Bora Bora anymore." (Be sure to pick someplace exotic and very different from wherever you are.) Of course, if the person next to you says, "Hey—I grew up in Bora Bora!" you are in some extremely serious trouble indeed. (See page 64 for easy exits.)

Other Excuse Lines

Some people prefer to keep an all-purpose survival quip at the tip of their tongues for when they trip up. One of the sample lines below may be just right for recovering from your next faux pas:

"Sorry—I haven't had any sleep."

"I'm jet-lagged."

"I'm not myself tonight; my wife [husband] left me yesterday." (This can double as a pickup line.)

"Do forgive me, I am very distracted by a problem [really big deal] at the office."

"Sorry; I had a really intense massage today and it's made me a little spacey."

"I can't think straight when in the presence of such physical perfection."

"I need new glasses. [I don't have my contacts in/I have drops in my eyes, etc.]"

"I'm really sorry; the truth is that someone (I don't want to tell you who) was just really rude to me and it's thrown me a bit. I haven't fully regained my equilibrium."

"That wasn't me; I'm channeling." (the New Age excuse)

Bad Excuses

Never, on the other hand, use any of the following explanations for your faux pas:

"I'm sho shorry . . . I think I've had too mush to drink."

"I can't help it . . . I . . . I . . . I want you."

"Sorry, I was abused as a child."

"I'm so bored I wasn't paying attention to what I was saying."

"The aliens made me say that [do that]."

THE HEALING POWER OF HUMOR

If you're like me, the first thing you want to do is employ a little humor to patch up an embarrassing moment. Everyone at the faux pas site needs a release from the tension: the faux pas maker, the faux pas-ee (if there is one), and especially any witnesses. And if the faux pas was a whopper and the fallout extreme (let's say, for instance, that the offended party has just slapped you in the face and left you standing with the party's hostess, the offended person's mate, and your mother-in-law), your only real hope might be humor.

While humor is always a bit risky—because it is so subjective—it can often completely neutralize the toxicity of the faux pas aftermath. Below are some "funny" responses—from the mildly ironic to the wildly silly—that might come in handy. If they don't go over brilliantly, at least they may serve to fill the deadly post–faux pas silence.

Please note: Not all of these lines will suit everyone, so pick the line or lines you think you would feel most natural using, or make up your own and record them in the spaces provided. The point is to have a line prerehearsed for faux pas emergencies. Most people in a crisis have trouble coming up with something funny on the spot.

Sample Lines

"I hate when that happens." (This line works best if in fact something very drastic and/or unusual has occurred, such as the aforementioned slap in the face.)

"English is my second language."

"Sorry—I was raised in a barn."

"You know how there are some days you should stay in bed? I think I'm having a whole year like that."

"You know how there are some days you should stay in bed? Well, I think I should have stayed in the womb."

"I didn't really say that, you know, that was just a clever ventriloquist throwing his voice."

"I just read a book on faux pas—that one is on page sixty-seven."

"That wasn't me—that was my wounded inner child."

"All right. I should be tortured, then shot, then tortured again."

(Talking into an imaginary communicator) *"Scotty, I'm having some trouble down here . . . Beam me up!"*

"

_____

_____
"

"

_____

_____
"

THE FAUX PAS-MOI: THE ART OF DENIAL

There is a memorable scene in the 1967 movie *A Guide for the Married Man* in which an unsuspecting wife comes home to find her husband in bed with another woman. There they are, caught in the act. The wife starts yelling, calling the husband a lying cheat, etc. Meanwhile, the other woman and the husband are calmly and quickly getting dressed. The husband, while putting on his clothes, responds innocently to the wife's berating with "What are you talking about, honey?" and "Now, just calm down and tell me what this is all about." The other woman, now fully dressed, leaves without saying a word, and the husband, cool and collected, finishes making the bed. No evidence remains of the rendezvous.

The wife, still angry, demands an explanation from her husband. "About what?" he says. "There was no one here. You've been working too hard, sweetheart."

Dazed, the wife sinks down on the bed. She is thinking maybe the whole thing never happened.

As ridiculous as this particular scene may be, it describes perfectly the essence of the spectacular Faux Pas-moi recovery technique. In the Faux Pas-moi, the idea is to deny the very occurrence of the faux pas. It may seem like a dangerous ploy, but the payoff can be big; and it is worth attempting when you are caught in truly horrible faux pas situations wherein the idea of trying to apologize or make excuses is not a palatable one.

There are four different ways to play out the Faux Pas-moi:

1. Pretend You Were Misunderstood

Suppose you've just committed a pretty bad faux pas, such as insulting a play or a book without realizing the person to whom you are waxing critical is the author. Perhaps the conversation has turned to a play that recently opened, a play called *The Horrible Mistake,* and you say something like, "I saw that play; it really dragged."

To your intense dismay, the man to your right gives you an irritated look and says to you, "Oh, really? I didn't think it dragged when I wrote it."

Sudden disaster. Okay. Take a second to breathe. Remain

calm. Do not allow humiliation to show on your face. Instead, look puzzled, and quickly think of the name of another play that is currently running.

"So you're the author of *Mayhem on Forty-second Street?*" you say. "Really? I thought a woman wrote that." Now, the playwright may be suspicious and suspect you are just trying to cover up your blunder. However, the real trick to the successful Faux Pas-moi is sticking to your denial position and refusing to cave in. Just say to yourself: Deny, deny, deny. It's like poker; you can't start to bluff and then change your mind halfway through the hand. (If you are not ready to go all the way with it, don't try this type of recovery at all.)

At this point the playwright will probably answer you dubiously with something like, "No, I wrote *The Horrible Mistake,*" as if to say, "Don't try to get out of it now," but remember: You must not fold! Keep insisting, "But I was talking about *Mayhem on Forty-second Street.* Isn't that what Joe was talking about?" This is a great technique when it works; sometimes you can manage to erase the mistake totally. The worst that can happen is that you "muff the bluff," and you are really not much worse off than you were before. After all, the injured playwright expects you to try to recover from such a blunder; the whole incident would probably be *more* insulting to him if you didn't make the effort. But perhaps he will believe your fervent denial. (His ego will want him to, in any case.)

2. Blame Someone Else

This may seem unethical, especially if we are talking about blaming a push or a drink spill on another person present, but don't rule it out. All's fair in love and embarrassment. Remember, however, that you can often blame an anonymous person. For example, in the case of the preceding playwright fiasco, you could try this:

"Oh no! You're the playwright? Oh my gosh. You're not going to believe this now, I know, but I never even *saw* the play. I was just trying to contribute to the conversation. I heard someone on the bus talking about it. That's the last time I pretend someone else's opinion is mine."

3. Pretend You Were Only Kidding

Perhaps you are talking to a woman you haven't seen in a while. Fatigue or alcohol or boredom has made you careless, and you say to her something like, "So, whatever happened to that jerk you used to date?" The minute the words leave your lips you have a bad feeling. And sure enough, she answers with a cold smile, "I married him."

Here's what you do: Keep that smile on your face; laugh, if you can, and say with appropriate merriment, "I know, silly. [Name of mutual friend at party] just told me. So where is he tonight?" And then if the person still looks offended: "Hey, can't you take a joke? Didn't you know I was kidding?"

4. Completely Ignore It

You have to be a cool customer to pull this off, but if you can do it, it's a no-muss/no-fuss way of effecting the Faux Pas-moi. Here's what you do—or, rather, what you don't do: Don't flinch, don't laugh, don't blush, don't acknowledge the faux pas in any way. Just erase it from your reality. It didn't happen. You didn't say it. You never did it. If you can act innocent enough, sometimes other people will begin to think they imagined the faux pas, or at least that whatever it was wasn't any big deal.

This form of the Faux Pas-moi is not just for daredevils; it is also for people who are too chicken or stunned to do anything about what has just taken place. Actually, the Faux Pas-moi is sometimes the easiest—maybe the only—dignified way to deal with what's happened.

For example, one day a woman I know named Sally went to one of those terribly cute restaurants where the rest rooms have confusing, arty symbols on them (often in the form of super-stylized hats or shoes or animals), and so through no fault of her own she suddenly found herself in the men's room. As soon as she entered, she saw a surprised (and occupied) man standing at a urinal. Sally felt that she had already come too far inside to leave gracefully. And so, unruffled, without blinking an eye, and ignoring the man's astonished stare, Sally quickly walked right up to one of the sinks, washed her hands, dried them with a paper towel, and walked back out. (She then proceeded to locate the women's room, where there was—naturally!—a long waiting line.)

Admittedly, Sally's boldness is an extreme illustration of the Faux Pas-moi, but it serves as a reminder that we must never underestimate the power we have at all times to create our own reality.

THE ANTI-RECOVERY

Sometimes faux pas are not only difficult to excuse or apologize away, but also impossible to bluff your way out of. One person I interviewed, Peter, told me of a harrowing moment at a reunion, similar to the preceding "jerk" faux pas. He was reminiscing with an old friend about a female classmate of theirs.

"That Gloria, she was always such an incredible ditz-brain," Peter said, laughing loudly.

The friend smiled icily and responded, "Gee, maybe I shouldn't be living with her."

Rather than try to somehow wriggle out of the mess he was in, Peter proceeded to use a version of what I call the Anti-recovery. Here's how it goes:

STEP ONE: *Do not retract your faux pas in any way: instead, restate your faux pas position.* Peter did this by saying honestly (looking surprised but not at all embarrassed), "Really? You're kidding! Wow. You know, I really *did* always think she was a bit ditzy."

STEP TWO: *Explain your faux pas remark or deed **without apologizing for it.*** Peter went on: "The reason I thought that was because in the tenth grade she spent a lot of time in the science lab melting lipsticks over the Bunsen burner."

STEP THREE: *Move gently away from your faux pas.* To complete his recovery, Peter continued calmly, "Obviously, though, she's not a ditz-brain if *you're* living with her. I guess I've misjudged her all these years. It just goes to show that you should never judge someone by what they did in the high school science lab!"

The Anti-recovery goes much further than the Faux Pas-moi. It says boldly: I have not made a mistake, and to prove it I will not only *not* apologize, I will *reaffirm* what I have said or done. This is a good approach for many category-two faux pas (in which you have been inadvertently mean) or category-five faux pas (wherein you have revealed yourself to be ignorant of something); if you actually emphasize that you don't know whatever it is you were expected to know, and refuse to be ashamed or apologetic, you can almost completely erase or counteract the faux pas.

P.S.: If you want to go all the way with the Anti-recovery, and you don't particularly care what people think of you, you can omit Step Three entirely.

DIVERSIONARY TACTICS

While the Anti-recovery may be one of the bravest and most spiritually pure methods of dealing with faux pas, I often prefer to go the cowardly, indirect route and create some kind of a diversion. Diversions work beautifully for mopping up after most mistakes, because everyone in the vicinity feels awkward and is looking for a quick way to end the tension. Creating a diversion, while it does not usually constitute total recovery, can move you and those around you swiftly away from the disaster area.

The Anecdotal Antidote

This particular technique—one of my all-time favorites—relies on the fact that everyone in the world has at some time made a really bad faux pas, and on the fact that in embarrassing situations, people look desperately for someone to pull them out of the social quagmire into which they have fallen. The only ingredient you need for your antidote is a superb faux pas story.

Let's say you have just made one of the worst and most common social errors, such as assuming a woman is someone's mother instead of his wife, or forgetting the name of the president of your company while introducing him. How can you distract your listeners and/or faux pas victim from your social ineptitude? Here's how: You simply acknowledge the mistake—with as little or as much chagrin as you want—and then say something like, "You know, if you think that was bad . . . " or "I am really the master of faux pas. Let me tell you what I did one time . . ." Then you proceed to recount your amusing faux pas anecdote. I have several particular stories of personal mishaps that I keep at the ready, just for this purpose.

For instance, there is one horrible repeat faux pas I make—something that happens to me over and over again, like a recurring nightmare. Every year I attend a New Year's Day party that the esteemed former mayor of New York City, David Dinkins, sometimes also attends. The first time I saw him there, I was having a very intense tête-à-tête with someone about living in Chicago. Suddenly I spotted Dinkins entering the room, and at the same time, a new person joined our twosome.

"Wow!" I exclaimed. "I can't believe that Harold Washington came to the party." Now, *I* knew that I had made this mistake only because my head was back in Chicago, and Harold Washington (who is now dead) had been the mayor when I lived there. But my listeners—especially the newcomer—didn't know this. I sounded like a complete idiot, or worse, like someone who can't tell one black mayor from another (cringe).

Ever since that excruciating experience, whenever I see Mayor Dinkins I remember my mistake and go into a state of complete paralysis. I can *never* remember his name—or mine. (One of the characteristics of faux pas is that once you have made a particular faux pas, it wears a kind of groove in your mind, and you will tend to follow the same path.) Last year, upon arriving at the party, the very first person I saw was the mayor. For some reason, he was in the kitchen, alone. Frozen in terror, I smiled inanely and said, "Hi!" Immediately we were joined by the seven-year-old daughter of one of my friends.

"Well, hello, Gina!" I said, embracing her. Suddenly it hit me: It was now my job, my duty, to introduce this inquisitive child to the illustrious former mayor. I commanded my brain to come up with the man's name. Nothing. A complete computer crash. I tried to stall for time. I became Mr. Rogers.

"Gina . . . do . . . you . . . know . . . who . . . *this* . . . is?!" (*I* certainly didn't.)

Both man and child were looking at me expectantly. I didn't want to introduce myself for fear my ignorance would become even more obvious. So I continued talking to Gina, praying with every fiber of my being that somehow I would be saved.

"This is . . . a *very* important man."

(Still nothing. Dinkins was looking a bit puzzled now.)

Finally I gave up. "This man used to be the *mayor of New York City!*" I announced with as much bravado as I could, and then I just fled, leaving Gina and the mayor alone in the kitchen, which was probably a great relief to them both.

People seem to love to hear this story, and it makes a good antidote because (1) it is a familiar story, as forgetting names is very common, (2) it is a celebrity story—always a plus when trying to divert anyone, (3) it is almost always worse than anything that is happening at the moment. (Note: The story should always be about something *you* did, if possible, because it is always less charming to talk about what some other dumbbell did. You don't want to appear to be comparing yourself favorably in a faux pas competition.)

The Anecdotal Antidote is a wonderful way to deal with your

faux pas without really dwelling on it, as well as a way to entertain and subtly apologize at the same time. In this manner you acknowledge your faux pas, but you also indicate clearly that it's certainly not the first time anybody slipped up, and it won't be the last.

Extreme Flattery

Flattery is always a powerful emergency weapon. My cousin Jenny once managed to smooth over a pretty bad blunder using this type of diversion. She had been invited to a party given by one of her colleagues, someone she didn't know very well but whom she wanted to know better. When she arrived she was let in to a fairly small, nicely decorated living room area with an adjoining kitchenette, and since she wanted so much to impress her hostess, she said immediately upon entering, "Oh, what a lovely apartment! You'll have to show me the rest of it." The colleague looked crestfallen.

"This is all there is," she answered.

Quickly Cousin Jenny scanned the room and located something to focus on. *"That couch!"* she exclaimed. "It's *gorgeous!* Wherever did you get it? I have been looking for something like that for *years.* Oh, I want it!"

As anyone whose feelings have ever been hurt can tell you, extreme flattery makes a good Band-Aid, if applied liberally and immediately after the wound has been inflicted. And even if it doesn't entirely take away the sting of an insult, flattery can feel so good that you forget about the pain for the time being.

This technique works especially well for recovering from category-three faux pas (accidental insults). Once I was telling a friend how much I enjoyed the book *The Hobbit.* After going on at some length, I added, "Though I would never confess this to any of my intellectual friends." My friend was, understandably, offended, but I recovered pretty nicely by spraying her right away with flattery: "Thank *heavens* I can be myself with you, someone who is smart but who isn't judgmental."

Other Diversionary Tactics

Sometimes just a simple change of subject can help your faux pas to fade away fast, especially if you use another recovery method first (such as an apology or the Faux Pas-moi). Abrupt lines such as "I'm starving! Let's go get some food," "Isn't that Susan Schwartz over there?" or "Look at that incredible car in front of us!" may help you make a speedy transition away from your faux pas. As with Extreme Flattery, you should use your surroundings to help find a diversionary focal point, and always remember that your faux pas casualty (or casualties) will usually be more than willing to be diverted from an embarrassing or awkward topic.

THE POST FAUX PAS FADE: EASY EXITS

Let's face it. Some moments, some faux pas are so disastrous, so agonizing, that you just want to get away from the people involved as quickly as possible. There is no recovering, there is only disappearing. For those times, you may want to use one of the quick-and-easy exits below. Please note: "EXIT" means either that you *immediately* separate from the people or person who witnessed your faux pas OR that you *immediately* leave the actual location altogether—the building, the house, the apartment, the restaurant, the office, or the planet.

"I have to go find something to help get my foot out of my mouth. Excuse me." EXIT.

"I think the best thing for me to do after that is just disappear. Excuse me." EXIT.

"Excuse me while I go kill myself." EXIT

"Excuse me while I go get a brain transplant." EXIT

"I'm going to just leave now, before I can do further damage." EXIT

"Pardon me, I have to go out and buy a new tongue." EXIT

RESPONDING AFTER THE FACT: TIME HEALS (SOME) WOUNDS

I am often haunted for days—sometimes even months or years—by some extremely horrendous blunder or other I made and did not successfully smooth over. This can occur either because my faux pas was of a superhuman kind of horribleness, or because I simply, for one reason or another, failed to recover—even partially—from my misdemeanor. And sometimes I don't even realize I have committed a faux pas until hours after the dreadful deed has been done!

If you find yourself waking up in the morning wondering how you can ever face so-and-so again, please do not despair. If you are willing to make the effort, you can often recover very nicely—*after the fact.* There are four avenues open to you after the fact: face-to-face; telephone; mail; and a gift. (Warning: Be certain that your faux pas was noticed before you try to recover after the fact. You might not want to turn yourself in for a crime that was overlooked.)

Face-To-Face

One of my friends (to protect the not-so-innocent, I'll call her Kate) told me of an awful experience she had involving an invitation. While out of town on business, Kate was looking forward to a scheduled dinner with person X. When X called her to arrange the specifics, it came up during the conversation that Kate was staying with another friend, Y. Though Y was only a passing acquaintance of X, X very graciously extended the invitation to include Y. Now, Kate did not particularly want Y coming with her to see X, so she simply said to X, "Thank you, I'll ask Y," and then didn't. Later, when she spoke again with X, she said that Y was unavailable for dinner.

Unfortunately for Kate, what she couldn't foresee was that Y would end up driving her to X's house, and then, since X wasn't home and had left the key under the mat, Y came in and waited with her. Kate got more and more nervous as the inevitable denouement approached. Indeed, it was not a minute after X and Y had said hello that X said to Y, "I was so sorry to hear from Kate that you won't be able to stay for dinner."

There wasn't much to be done under the circumstances. Y looked confused for a moment, then forced a smile, said goodbye, and left. Kate tried the rest of the night to assuage her guilt by overeating.

Kate's hurtful faux pas was one of those that just cannot be dealt with at the faux pas scene itself. However, when Kate saw Y again, she brought up the incident, apologized profusely, and explained that she had not extended X's invitation to Y because she had wanted quality time with X, but that she should have been up front with X about her wishes in the first place.

There are definitely situations in which it is hopeless to attempt any faux pas recovery at the moment it occurs, and it is also not unrealistic to assume that there will be times when you may be too stunned, scared, embarrassed, confused, tired, or tipsy to do anything other than stare in unblinking horror at the blurred faces around you. In these cases, it is best to attend to the faux pas repair work later on. Meanwhile, though the waiting period may be uncomfortable, keep in mind that you can and will undo the damage when you next see the person, using one or more of the recovery methods in this chapter.

The advantage to holding off on your recovery until you see the person again is that the horror of your faux pas will have faded somewhat (even if you see the person the next day) and there will be less emotion around it. This makes the wound or the bad impression easier to heal or to reverse. If you are going to recover after the fact, doing it face-to-face is the most preferable method, because you can ascertain whether or not your apology or excuse is working, and adjust your manner or words accordingly. Also, it is more casual than the following three alternatives.

Telephoning

If it was a bad enough faux pas to warrant it, and you just want to take your medicine and get it over with, you could phone the person and grovel, lie, or explain yourself over the wire. If Kate hadn't seen Y again before she left town, she would have done this almost as soon as she got back home. This is pretty courageous and can be about as much fun as getting a wart burned off, but it is usually well worth it and you will feel better afterward.

If I don't want to make a big deal about my faux pas—and if I suspect the other person didn't notice it—I have been known to call the person up on another pretext, and then casually, as obliquely as I can, bring the conversation around to the faux pas. If the person doesn't respond to any of my hints, I usually count myself lucky and leave it alone.

Letter Writing

This after-the-fact practice is somewhat old-fashioned but often works beautifully. People are often touched to receive a hand-written note that says something like:

> *"I am writing to beg your pardon. I believe I was inadvertently rude to you at Sotheby's last Thursday. It was completely un-intentional, though extremely unmannerly of me nonetheless. Please accept my sincere apology."*

Remember, however, that it is considered extremely formal nowadays to write this kind of note (so much so that your mis-sive could be mistaken for a joke), and that once you write something down, you can never take it back. Clever cards—ones designed for apologies—are another matter. They make excellent after-the-fact salves. They are less formal and can be chosen to fit the specific incident, and you need write only a few words, such as "Sorry for my silly blunder," at the bottom.

Gift Giving

For the most severe faux pas, you may want to resort to gift giv-ing, otherwise known as bribery. To a person whose wig you ac-cidentally pulled off in full view of fifty people, expensive flowers are probably the only way to go (but not red roses, please. They are too romantic in feeling). For other, slightly less deplorable transgressions, you can tailor the gift, if you like, to the circumstances. I once sent a nice fountain pen to someone whose linen tablecloth I soiled with ink. (Never write down your address for someone on a thin piece of paper on top of the dinner table!) My note read, "Next time you see me I promise to wear my white formal, and you can squirt this all over me. Sorry about your lovely tablecloth—please do accept my sincere apologies."

FAUX PAS-CIFISTS: SOCIAL SUPERHEROES

If there's one thing that warms my heart, it's watching a faux pas-cifist, or faux pas angel, at work. A faux pas-cifist is a witness, a bystander, or a third party who accurately perceives a faux pas situation and steps in unselfishly to save the day. Of course, often the faux pas victim himself is kind enough to help the faux pas perpetrator over his embarrassment, but it's another thing altogether when an individual who would otherwise not be directly involved offers assistance. These people are no less than the heroes and heroines of the social universe.

A few years ago my friend Amy and I were having a very intense tête-à-tête while standing in a long movie line on Manhattan's upper east side. Now, when you live in New York City you get used to discussing the intimate details of your life in the midst of strangers, because, frankly, if you didn't, you'd never talk anywhere but inside your apartment. You learn to think of strangers both as people and as part of the scenery; you tend to ignore the fact that on the subway twenty people are listening to every word you say. Unfortunately, this practice can sometimes lead to trouble, and in this case caused me to forget one of the major rules of avoiding faux pas (see Chapter 2), namely: *Be aware at all times of who is within earshot.*

I was filling Amy in on a date I had had with a very "hot" guy. (He worked in the financial industry but also cooked and taught yoga.) Just when I was saying, "Rich is really nice, seems really centered and healthy and all, except the one thing I can't figure out is that all his friends I met at this party we went to were so *incredibly* boring," I happened to turn around and glance at the person behind me, who looked vaguely familiar and was, of course, none other than one of the incredibly boring friends in question. (When will I ever learn that New York is just another small town?) There was no doubt in my mind that he had heard me; he was wearing a very hurt, angry expression and turned the other way when I looked at him.

When I realized that not only had I insulted this man but also that he had heard me gushing on and on about my date with his friend, I felt like knocking myself on the head until I was unconscious. I just sank into Amy, closed my eyes, and put my head on her shoulder, too mortified to try to perform the Faux Pas-moi or any other recovery technique. I felt completely and utterly doomed. The worst thing was that we were trapped in the movie line, so I couldn't even make a quick exit.

Luckily for me, however, the woman who was with the "boring man" stepped in unexpectedly. "Excuse me," she said, tapping me on the shoulder. I had no alternative; I turned around. "I think I met you at the party on Saturday." She smiled and went on in a very composed manner. "I couldn't help overhearing what you were saying—you know, big parties really *can* be boring, especially if you don't know anybody there." She smiled again. Both the boring man and I clung to her every word; she was our lifeline. She smiled even wider and said, "Especially if you are with someone new whom you really want to get to know. Rich *is* really nice, isn't he?" I blushed, but smiled back, gratefully. Then she indicated the boring man. "Did you meet Joe?" Blushing even deeper, I mumbled, "I'm not sure." I introduced Amy, and then the fabulous Faux Pas-cifist, whose name turned out to be Lila, led us all in a nice four-way conversation. Joe was stiff at first, but I made sure I was especially nice to him and acted supremely interested in everything he said. By the time the line began moving I felt that Joe believed I did not really think he was boring, and that he knew I was not a total jerk and he was not going to run and tell Rich that I was one. Considering the enormity of the faux pas, it was a major—if not total—recovery, and I owed it all to Lila.

Lila was a master Faux Pas-cifist. There are not that many people who could and would handle the above situation with as much finesse and generosity. Most Faux Pas-cifists are lesser but still admirable people who might help others recover from faux pas using a simple recovery line. ("Don't mind Charley; he's a new parent—he's had about five seconds sleep today.") A Faux Pas-cifist will take over for someone who is floundering during an introduction and fill in the missing name(s) or qualifiers. Another common strategy of your garden-variety Faux Pas-cifist is one of diversion; the kind interloper sees someone in trouble and fills the awkwardness with a change of subject or a funny comment.

For a person who makes as many faux pas as I do, all forms of faux pas-cifism are a godsend. With the kindness of strangers—as well as a bag full of recovery tricks—we should all be able to survive whatever the faux pas Fates hand us.

..... 4 .....

OTHER FAUX PAS
AND TAILORED
RECOVERY LINES

■ ■ ■ ■ ■ ■ ■ ■ ■ ■

IN ADDITION to relying on the basic recovery techniques, I have found it also quite advantageous to have on hand some made-to-order recovery lines for surviving specific faux pas. For one thing, some people can memorize lines easier than they can remember maneuvers. Moreover, many people tend to make the same kind of mistake often, such as during introductions, and can use a version of the same line over and over to get them out of trouble.

While all of the faux pas that follow could be handled by employing one of the recovery techniques described in the last chapter, it is sometimes easier, during that mind-freezing faux pas aftermath, to rely on a rehearsed stock line that you won't have to think about too much. Naturally, if none of these recovery lines fits your taste or circumstances, they can and should be modified to fit the occasion as well as your personal style. (Please note: Total recovery is a rare accomplishment. Most of these lines will help you effectively *survive* the faux pas—they will ease the tension, dispel the embarrassment, smooth over the insult—and help you move on. But don't expect miracles. You can't go back in time.)

HELLO, GOOD-BYE: GREETING GOOFS AND MISTAKES DURING DEPARTURE

Hellos

Introductions are most people's worst nightmare. Flubbing names during introductions is such a common faux pas, in fact, that some experts have given this particular lack of social grace a clinical term: dysnomnesia. Dysnomnesia afflicts everyone at one time or another. (I've had plenty of my own attacks of dysnomnesia, and once even introduced myself to Erica Jong as Erica Jong. Boy, was she confused!) Either you can't remember the person's name, you use an incorrect qualifier (e.g., "and this is her husband," when the two people are not married), or you actually start a conversation before you realize you have mistaken the person for someone else.

Whatever form your greeting goof takes, one thing is certain: The more important it is that you get it right, the more likely it is that you are going to get it wrong. So whether you've just forgotten your boss's name or your own, here are some lines that may help alleviate the situation:

Recovery Lines

"I'm so sorry; I have a name disorder called dysnomnesia. Really. I've been diagnosed by a name disorder specialist—Dr. . . . Dr. . . . what's his name."

"I've never been able to remember names; it runs in my family. At family reunions there are generally a lot of 'Hey, yous.'"

"Whoops, I'm afraid I thought you were Bob Tompkins. Well, we were obviously meant to talk together. There are no accidents in life, right?"

Good-byes

You're less likely to stumble when leaving a conversation, but it still happens. You might make the mistake of saying, "So nice to meet you," when in fact you have met several times before, and what you meant to say was, "So nice to see you again." Sometimes you just say something ridiculous upon leaving someone's house, like, "Thanks. The food and the bathrooms were great." One friend of mine was saying good-bye to his father on the phone and could not remember the name of his father's new wife. He ended up starting, "And say hello to . . ." and then just stopped awkwardly in midsentence. I have often totally crumbled saying good-bye to a date at the door. (Once I mumbled, "See you tomorrow," when we had no such plan.)

As always, if you are tipsy, or are feeling nervous or embarrassed already, these good-bye goofs are more likely to occur. Here are some proven good-bye-goof recovery lines to try:

Recovery Lines

"Did I say 'Nice to meet you'? Of course, I meant to say 'So nice to see you again.' I guess every time we talk it's so interesting, it's as if we are talking for the first time!"

"I guess it really is time for me to leave!"

"Wait a minute, maybe I should stay for another drink so I can really embarrass myself."

"I hate to say good-bye to you—so I decided to prolong it by making a faux pas."

OBSERVATION WRECKS: APPEARANCE FAUX PAS

Commenting on someone's appearance is dangerous—the virtual high dive of the social realm. Even the apparently safe "You've lost so much weight!" can send someone into tears if the reason for the weight loss is that the person is suffering from a debilitating illness. (If there is no way for you to know this, it's not *technically* a faux pas. But appearance observations by their nature are all borderline faux pas.) Even seemingly innocent remarks can suddenly transform themselves into insults. For example, once at a friend's wedding, I greeted the friend's mother with "You look beautiful today," and then spent the next sixty seconds assuring her that, of course, she *always* looked beautiful, but particularly so on this momentous occasion. Much more disastrous was the time I witnessed an acquaintance of mine, a woman named Miriam, inform another woman that she had a speck of dirt on her face—it was a well-meaning observation intended to help, so that the unsightly thing could be surreptitiously removed. Blushing deeply, the speck-sporting woman informed Miriam that the offending mark was, in fact, a scab.

Common observation wrecks include observations about: pregnancy, weight, hair, facial marks, and clothing; as well as observations about your surroundings (e.g., "Who made this disgusting cake! Oh, whoops. Sorry.").

Recovery Lines

"Forgive me. I need new glasses. And new manners."

"I'm terribly sorry, it's really not noticeable. I was just looking for conversation, which I'm very bad at."

"Look: I swear to you that it isn't that your body looks pregnant. It's your face—it's positively radiant, and I usually see that much glow only in pregnant women. So . . . what's making you so happy?"

"You made this [item of food]? Oh God, I am so embarrassed. To tell you the truth, I am a very bad judge of cuisine—everyone tells me that. I am ashamed to say I am used to store-bought, preservative-filled food substitutes. For all I know this could be the best [item of food] ever made."

"That didn't come out quite right. Please believe me, I meant it as a compliment."

THE HOSTESS WITHOUT THE MOSTEST

When I think back on some of the things I have said and done at parties I have given, it makes me shudder. While I have never actually danced on top of my coffee table with a lampshade on my head, I have, for instance, announced to some of my first arrivals at a cocktail party that I was "afraid no one would come." (So what were *they*, chopped liver?) I have also been known to make people feel guilty when they left early ("Oh no! You're *not* leaving already!?"). One time I threw a party and invited a friend and his new wife as well as his still-suffering jilted ex-girlfriend. (It wasn't pretty.)

Other host faux pas include: inviting to a dinner party two people whom you have forgotten you fixed up together on a disastrous blind date; accidentally letting a guest know he really hadn't been invited; pressing a drink on a recovering alcoholic; or talking about other parties you've had to which some people weren't invited.

Note: With some hostess faux pas, it may be advisable not to try to recover until after the fact, especially when it comes to mistakes of mixing the wrong people together. Any emphasis on your blunder at the actual event serves only to make matters worse.

Recovery Lines

"I'm such a terrible hostess. Giving parties makes me nervous."

"I'm so excited to have this many of my favorite people all together that I don't know what I'm doing!"

(After the fact)
"I must apologize for our insensitivity about the guest list. I found out

that my husband had already invited him, *but of course, we really wanted to have* you. *But it was too late to uninvite him."*

GUEST FAUX PAS

Sometimes the hostess is perfect and it's the guests who misbehave. One man I know invited eight people to a seven-o'clock dinner party and no one arrived until eight-fifteen! At another dinner party I attended, several guests actually had the bad manners to complain that the host had prepared rice and beans as the main course. Once a houseguest of mine offered to cook dinner for me and four of my friends and then forced me to go out and purchase pasta bowls. (I learned the hard way that Italian men will *not* serve pasta on plates.) Sometimes someone will drop by who is not even invited, barging in on you while you are trying to wallpaper the den. And then there's the old standard: someone comes to your house, gets rip-roaring drunk, and proceeds to insult you or your friends, or smash something.

If you are responsible for a Guest Faux Pas of this magnitude, you may want to send flowers or a gift the next day, in conjunction with a version of one of the recovery lines below. Never forget that too much alcohol almost guarantees the production of faux pas.

Of course, the catch-22 of the Guest Faux Pas is that the offender seldom knows he has done anything wrong. However, for those rare, repentant guests:

Recovery Lines
"Okay, cross me off your future guest lists."

"That was rude; I'm sorry. Can I scrub your kitchen floor with a toothbrush or something to make up for it?"

"Tell you what, next time you come to my house you can break a vase or throw wine on the carpet."

"A famous person once said, 'A host is like a general; it takes a mishap to reveal his genius.' Well, it's time to start revealing your genius."

(slapping yourself) *"Bad guest! Bad!"*

"I beg your pardon. I probably shouldn't be allowed to socialize with normal people."

"I'm really sorry. Next time I have a party, you have my permission to ruin it."

"I just wanted to help make your party memorable."

■ ■ ■

PRESENTS OF MIND: GIFT FAUX PAS

I admit to being completely uninterested in the rules and regulations of when you should bring a gift, how long a time period you have in which to send a wedding or baby gift, what kind of thank-you note to use, etc. What *can* be terrifying (and therefore more important to talk about) are those times when something unexpected and dreadful happens at the moment the gift is given.

The practice of gift giving is fraught with faux pas-ibilities, mainly because there is a high level of emotion surrounding most gift exchanges. For this reason both the giver and the receiver usually try to stick to the accepted, boring-but-safe gift comments, such as: "I hope you like it," or "What a wonderful gift! Thank you." Unfortunately, this high emotional state is also the reason this prudent practice often falls by the wayside. People do tend to blurt out the wrong thing when they are nervous or excited. In fact, not too long ago, my friend Samantha committed one of the worst gift faux pas you can make. (She swears that the experience taught her a lesson and that she'll never again make the same mistake.)

It was at a baby shower. After the mother-to-be had opened Samantha's gift, Samantha started talking loudly and at great length about these "horrible, unbelievably pretentious" Christian Dior baby outfits she had seen while shopping, and how "nobody she knew would even *think* about getting such over-priced status symbols for a baby." She went on and on, as one does sometimes. Thirty minutes later, when the inevitable Christian Dior baby outfit was unwrapped, Samantha remembers turning quietly to the woman next to her and saying, "I wish God would just take me now."

Gift Faux Pas can be committed by the person who is receiving a present or by the one who is giving it. Sometimes, without meaning to, you let it be known that you already own an identical item, or simply that you don't like it, or won't use it. Once, to my intense dismay, the recipient of one of my gifts informed me she had read the gift was defective and I should take it back to the store and get my money back! Sometimes the gift giver will let it slip that he didn't pay much for the gift; that the gift is something somebody gave to him and he's passing it on to you (this is known as the recycled gift); or that while *you* will probably like the item, it is by no means something he would have acquired for himself. On the other hand, sometimes the receiver's well-meaning response, "Thanks! I would *never* buy one of these for myself," can also be taken the wrong way. Once I witnessed a major mess-up: when a woman exclaimed upon opening a present, "Oh, I know someone who will just love this!"

Always remember, before opting for one of these recovery lines, that the Faux Pas-moi (see page 54) is often the best way to go.

Recovery Lines

(For the gift receiver)

"Just wrap me up with this paper and send me COD to the School for Good Manners."

"I'm so glad I know you; you always give me such wonderful, interesting gifts. In spite of my weird reactions to them."

"Actually, now that I look at this up close . . . it's really beautiful. I can't wait to use it [wear it/hang it/eat it]."

(After making the comment "I know someone who will just love this"): *". . . I can't wait to show it to her—she'll be green with envy!"*

(For the gift giver)

"It's just that I couldn't carry it off. I'm not as attractive [creative/ brave/formal, etc.] as you. But I'll live vicariously through your having it."

"Actually, that Dior baby outfit is really lovely. I don't know what I was talking about. I think I was feeling guilty that I didn't buy one. I've always been insecure about my fashion sense."

"No . . . I didn't mean that I didn't pay a lot for it, only that I shopped around and got it at a good price."

SEXUAL FAUX PAS

According to the *Oxford English Dictionary*, the word *faux pas* originally (in the 1600s) referred to a woman's "lapse in virtue" and only later began to be used to describe less intimate social errors. Today, bedroom faux pas encompass quite a range of matters. The faux pas you can commit include everything from accidentally making an unflattering comment about your partner's anatomy to calling out the wrong name at an inopportune moment. Many boudoir boo-boos are so mortifying (in an intensely intimate way) that they can't be discussed here. Of course, sexual faux pas also occur outside the bedroom; for example, you might be overheard talking about sex by the wrong person (like a nun, or your doorman.)

Sexual faux pas of any kind carry a double dose of humiliation, because there is (unfortunately) so much shame and embarrassment in this area already. The average sexual faux pas is therefore particularly difficult to overcome. Somewhat less excruciating is the double entendre, which accounts for a large part of the world's sexual faux pas. Some of these can be fairly embarrassing while others border on the cute. My mother, when she was newly married, was asked by a gentleman friend of her mother-in-law's how married life was going, and she—nervous and trying a little too hard to be witty—cheerfully replied, "Oh, I'm keeping my end up." This caused my mother to blush and the gentleman to cough until he almost choked. (As you can see, the making of faux pas seems to run in my family.)

A not-so-adorable slip was made by a friend of mine while visiting the parents of his gay lover for the first time. The situation was somewhat awkward for all involved; the lover had recently come out to his family, and frankly they weren't too thrilled about it. However, they generously put their son and his partner in the best guest bedroom, which had in it a queen-size bed covered with a beautiful, hand-made quilt. The first day after they had arrived, the mother popped in to see how the couple was doing. Ever anxious to please, my friend leapt off the bed, smiled grandly, and said, "Oh, Mrs. ———, we've certainly been enjoying your quilt!"

Recovery Lines (For double entendres)

(After laughing) *"I believe that was what is referred to as a double entendre, otherwise known as a faux pas. I wonder why we always use French to refer to anything embarrassing."*

"Oops. Maybe they should hire me to talk on one of those one-nine-hundred lines."

"I know Freud says there are no accidents, but I swear I didn't mean that the way it sounded."

Recovery Lines (For boo-boos in the boudoir)
"Oh, Honey, you were just hearing things. I've read that that happens to [men/women] during sex."

"That was the name of my third wife. Or was it my fourth?"

"Sorry, sex makes me insane. I don't know what I'm saying."

"What can you expect? All the blood from my brain has gone you-know-where."

"I'm just testing your love for me. If you don't get up and walk out after that, you are true blue."

"My lips may say one thing, but my heart—as well as the rest of my body—is saying another."

(After a faux pas of a particularly physical nature): *"Oops, sorry. I shouldn't have tried that. I was trying to impress you by getting fancy."*

"Oh, was that your hair? I thought you were screaming from pleasure."

CURSES, FOILED AGAIN: BAD LANGUAGE SLIPS AND BREAKING TABOOS

I used to work in an office with people who used pretty bad language. I got so accustomed to hearing (and employing) the "F word" that when I went to visit my relatives, I had to prep myself on the train so that I wouldn't shock them all into fainting fits with my atrocious New Yorker sewer mouth.

In general, it really is a good idea to refrain from using bad language—at any time. As someone famous once said, "Cursing is for people who can't find the words to express themselves." In any case, before using any "foul" language, you must be *absolutely certain* the company you are in can stomach it. When you swear in the wrong circumstances (at a business dinner or at a religious ceremony, for example) it can be like suddenly having a scarlet letter on your forehead—you feel morally bankrupt and are sure that at any moment you'll be stoned by angry villagers. When you use what is deemed to be inappropriate profanity you are breaking one of society's taboos.

There are other incidents of inappropriate behavior that have a similar taboo-breaking feeling. Once my friend Mary was having a conversation with an acquaintance about karate; he was trying to explain the power of a hard karate kick. Mary, greatly interested, asked him in front of a large group of people just how a karate kick to the solar plexus compared to getting kicked in the balls. There was a long silence at the table before he addressed the question. (It turned out that a karate kick to the solar plexus is just as painful but knocks you out completely.) Mary realized too late that the subject of testicle kicking was not appropriate to the company she was in.

Whether or not you are crossing the line in these areas of "moral" behavior is always extremely subjective—it really depends where you are. Most of the following recovery lines rely on that fact.

Recovery Lines

"I am so sorry. I have a boss [husband/wife/friend/associate] who swears constantly and I'm afraid I've picked up his/her bad habit. It's one I must break."

"Where did that come from? Some other person—probably a sailor—took over my body for a second."

"Just seeing whether anyone was listening."

"Gosh, that didn't come out of my mouth right. Anybody got any soap?"

"I didn't really say that, did I? Someone please get me some tape for my mouth."

OFFICE OFFENSES

The workplace is a dangerous domain in which to make faux pas; too many big ones and you might just be out of a job. Actually, most Office Offenses happen during job interviews. For example, during one memorable interview, my sister-in-law was asked about what hours she preferred working. After explaining she wanted to work only part-time, and in a misguided effort at female bonding, my sister-in-law replied, "Believe me, I'm *not* one of those women who makes her children suffer so she can work all the time." The full-time working mom who was the interviewer merely looked at my sister-in-law over the top of her glasses and kindly let the comment slide. (Note: None of the lines below is to be used in interview situations. If you make a faux pas during an interview, it's best to ignore it [see the Faux Pas-moi, page 54]).

Office Offenses usually occur when you assume things about other people in the company or when you behave in a way that is inappropriate for an office setting. You might mistake the vice president of a company for the new intern. You might tell someone how sorry you are about his termination before he has received his pink slip. You might even forget yourself and blurt out at a staff meeting that you had sex last night for the first time in months. (And I know of at least one person who was caught in the act of photocopying his face—not to mention other body parts—on the copy machine.)

Here are a few lines to help you survive those bad faux pas days at the office:

Recovery Lines

"As you may suspect, I've been sent by the competition to mess things up."

"I guess my interpersonal skills need some work."

"Oops. Sorry—I should probably sign over my paycheck to you for that!"

(After a particularly bad offense in front of your boss) *"I smell a promotion!"*

or

"I guess this wouldn't be the perfect time to talk about my raise."

RESTAURANT AND FOOD FAUX PAS

As a Manhattanite of some thirteen years, I have eaten out a lot. I have tripped waiters, insulted cooks, and eaten other people's food by mistake. I never can remember what my waiter looks like—or even what sex he or she is. I've often asked a man if he is our waiter when it was a woman who was waiting on us. One time I took a friend out for his birthday, and then, by the end of dinner, I forgot I was taking him out and presented him presumptuously with his portion of the bill. I have witnessed dinner party participants embarrassing themselves by criticizing a wine they mistakenly thought was one *they* brought. I have looked on in disbelief as a bumptious bumbler lambasted a dessert he thought was made by a college buddy of his (with whom he had a history of this kind of sparring) when it was made by the buddy's wife.

There are hundreds of different faux pas one can make when dining out; luckily, the setting of a restaurant or dinner table lends itself easily to some fine after-faux-pas vintage lines:

"It must be something they put in the food."

"Oh well, you didn't want to come back to this place anyway, did you?"

"Don't let me have any more wine [chocolate]. It's going to my head."

"Darn. I'm going to have to find a new state for my business lunches."

"You know, Zagat's has a special index for this, called 'Restaurants that [your name] can never go back to again.'"

(To your table, after tripping a waiter):
"Whoops. I forgot you're supposed to tip them, not trip them."

"You can dress me up, but you can't take me out—not to a restaurant [dinner party] anyway!"

"Check, please!"

HEALTH AND HOSPITAL HORRORS

There are few places on earth more nerve-racking than hospitals. I personally enter an altered state the minute I am in a hospital. I immediately become paranoid, hypersensitive, and altogether jittery. While not everyone is the neurotic mess I am, most people are fairly faux pas–prone when in hospitals, often because they are aware that they mustn't say anything to upset the sick people who are there. Even my friend Jeff, who is now a doctor, described an awkward moment in an AIDS hospice where he used to work:

"I had just entered the room and was making a real effort to be cheerful and positive, and I looked around the room and said, 'Oh, how great—a hat rack!' Of course, the item was not a hat rack but an IV stand. I felt like lying down in the bed next to the patient and burying my face in the pillow."

I used to make the following type of gaffe continually: I'd see a woman on crutches and would say something like, "Oh, how awful it must be to have to go to work on crutches!" (thinking it was a temporary injury). The person's injury would invariably be chronic and serious. Never assume! You just never know; I was told a supposedly true hospital horror story about someone looking through the window at the newborn babies and saying to a woman next to her, "Isn't it amazing that they come out so perfectly, that they are born with all their fingers and toes and everything?" You guessed it: The woman to whom she was speaking said, "Mine wasn't."

Recovery Lines

"I am so sorry; hospitals make me so anxious that I tend to lose control of my mouth."

"I am trying to distract you with my ineptitude."

"I bet you really want out of here so you won't have any more people coming in here and making you feel worse."

"I'm so glad to see you looking so well that it's made me drunk with relief."

"Maybe I should have just sent a card."

"More painkillers?"

THE PHONE PAS: BLUNDERS ON THE TELEPHONE

My father once told me that my grandfather used to answer the telephone by yelling, "What do you want?" into the receiver. He wasn't a tyrant; it's just that he wasn't accustomed to using the phone and didn't quite understand the etiquette. Today the average person spends much of his life on the phone, and the conversational rules are similar to those of face-to-face interaction. You can make most of the same faux pas over the phone as you can in person. There are some, however, that can be made *only* on the phone. These are called Phone Pas.

Most Phone Pas fall into one of three groups. The first is when you are short or even rude to someone who calls because you think that the person is a telemarketer looking to sell you a credit card or home delivery of the local newspaper. These cases of mistaken identity often happen because the caller mispronounces your name. It's amazing how sarcastic and contemptuous you can be before you finally discover that it's, say, the White House on the line.

The second type of Phone Pas occurs when you leave an idiotic message on an answering machine. (Indeed, answering machines are by their very nature faux pas magnets, you are on the spot, you are being taped, and you will *never* be able to take it back. I feel that most faux pas committed on answering machines really don't count, they are so inescapable.)

The third kind of Phone Pas are wrong-number connections that go on too long. For example, one of the people interviewed for this book told me a delightful story about calling someone to sing "Happy Birthday" to him over the phone. Since the "birthday boy" lived alone, as soon as the well-wisher heard the receiver being picked up, he began to sing, in full voice and with a loud, drawn-out *and many more!* at the end. When he finally stopped singing, instead of the appreciative voice of his friend, he heard a confused woman's voice asking him who he was. He had dialed the wrong number. What was really confusing was that by a bizarre coincidence, it was also the birthday of the woman's husband!

Recovery Lines

"I'm so sorry. I thought you were MCI calling; they call me about four times a day and it's driving me crazy."

"Wait a minute—I didn't say that; there must be someone else on this line!"

"They can invent call waiting, call answering, and call forwarding, but they will never invent call editing."

(In a Humphrey Bogart voice) *"All the numbers of all the phones in the world, and I dialed yours!"*

"Oops, sorry. I thought I had called my brother. Just pretend this was a dream."

"I dialed the wrong number? Maybe you answered the wrong phone!"

"Well . . . okay . . . I guess I have the wrong number. So what are you doing Friday night?"

"Hi. I just wanted you to know about this person who has been calling people I know and impersonating me on answering machines, saying all kinds of stupid things . . ."

FAUX PAS IN WRITING

This breed of faux pas is relatively rare, for the simple reason that you usually have ample time to think before you write down anything. In addition, nobody writes letters these days (although E-mail has brought back letter writing in a different form). The other thing about Faux Pas in Writing is that many times you will never know you have made them. The letter is gone, and unless you have a copy or the person in receipt of your written faux pas mentions it, you will remain in blessed ignorance.

I did hear of one painful written faux pas, however. It happened when a veterinarian sent a hand-signed form letter to one of his customers, informing her that it was time for her dog, Spiro's, annual checkup. Unfortunately, Spiro had been put to sleep by that very vet not two months before! Obviously this was a clerical error, but it was still an inexcusable faux pas that caused emotional distress to the letter's recipient.

Other matters you can mangle by mail include: spelling someone's name wrong; putting the wrong letter in the wrong envelope; enclosing a copy of something you didn't mean to enclose; and disclosing information that you find out after mailing the letter you shouldn't have disclosed. As infrequent as they are, mistakes by mail are so powerful (never put anything in writing, as the saying goes) that they almost always require an apology or explanation by phone—or even in person. One of the lines below may help bail you out of your next inscribed indiscretion.

Recovery Lines

"About my letter: Can you do me a favor and burn the darn thing? In fact, maybe we could perform some sort of ritual to make the whole incident go away."

"I believe my assistant might have accidentally enclosed something for someone else in your package. I've got him on bread and water. Would you mind just throwing it away and forgetting you got it?"

For E–mail:
"Sorry—cyberspace terrorists got into my files."

DEATH BLOWS: WHEN SOMEONE HAS PASSED AWAY (AND YOU WISH YOU WOULD, TOO)

The memory of some of my most hideous faux pas can still cause me queasiness, even though they may have taken place long ago. One of these unhappy incidents happened more than fifteen years ago, in Baltimore, where I grew up.

I was working at the time for the mother of a friend of mine from high school. (Tragically, this friend had been run over and killed by a car in Europe a few years before.) The mother was wonderful to me—she had not only given me the job but also picked me up in the morning to go to work, as we lived near to each other.

One morning I was late. I dashed out of the house and ran to where Mrs. _____ was accustomed to waiting for me. Because I was in a hurry, I was somewhat cavalier in crossing the street and had to make a mad dash in front of an oncoming car. Breathless but cheerful, I jumped into Mrs. _____'s car and said, "Wow! Sorry I'm late. Did you see me almost get hit by that car?"

The words just hung in the air, like some toxic chemical bomb that had exploded unexpectedly in our faces. All breathing in the car stopped. At last Mrs. _____ said crisply, "Yes. I certainly did." We both knew how sorry I was I had said it, but there was no taking it back.

Faux pas concerning subject of death are even worse than sexual faux pas. Death is our deepest, darkest fear, and any crossing over the line on this area is shattering to people's equilibrium. Whether you've just made a bad "dead joke" at a funeral or you've made an insensitive comment about dying to a recent mourner, you may be able to lessen the horror of these deadly faux pas with one of the following lines. (Warning: If you have just dealt a Death Blow faux pas, please resist all urges to try to fix things up with "deadly" jokes such as: "That was a killer faux pas" or "That comment really buried [slayed] me," or you really will be committing social suicide.)

Recovery Lines

"Oh my God. (pause) Well, I didn't mean to bring up a painful subject; but as long as I have—how are you doing these days?"

"I'm sorry, that was in bad taste. I don't deal with death very well; it makes me say things I don't really mean."

"I'm sorry. I was so terrified that I'd end up saying something just like that, that that's just what I did."

"I know [name of dead person] up in heaven will forgive me; I hope you can, too. That was a dumb thing to say."

SLIP OF THE YOUNG: WHEN YOUR CHILD MAKES A FAUX PAS

It was one of those parties where it was almost a blessing that everyone had had too much to drink.

Fred and Ginny had invited Fred's business partner to dinner, along with several other people. As it happened, that very day they had been discussing this business partner, whose name is Jim, in front of their eight-year-old son. Fred had made the joke that Jim's recent lecture at a conference was so bad that he had gotten a "sitting ovation." Later that evening, as dessert was being served, Jim was bragging about how well he had done at the conference. The eight-year-old spoke up. "Yeah, Uncle Jim," he said innocently, "I heard you were so good you got a sitting ovation!"

This kind of Slip-of-the-Young faux pas is unfortunately unavoidable if you gossip about other people in front of your children. But even if you don't, kids will come out with some very hurtful zingers, simply because they haven't got their social filters in place yet. Is this kind of honesty a more spiritually pure path than courtesy-driven deceit? Perhaps, but when your child asks your new nanny why she is so fat, you may need one of these recovery lines:

Recovery Lines (These are best delivered after your child has left the room)

"Oh, that Suzie. She's always misquoting me in the most embarrassing manner! What I actually said is . . ."

"I do apologize. He didn't mean anything by that—actually he says that to just about everyone."

"You know, sometimes children say the darndest things!"

"You know, sometimes what children say reflects what their parents think, and then again, sometimes—like now—I think they are just repeating something they heard on TV."

THE JOKING GUN: WHEN HUMOR BACKFIRES

Many of the recovery lines in this chapter are meant to be humorous (ranging from the witty to the silly). Humor is one of the best tools we have for repairing tears in our social fabric. Humor gone awry, however, can be one of the worst things to happen to you.

Picture this. You are on a train. The woman seated next to you is nice-looking and perfectly coiffed. You begin a conversation, and she is beginning to warm up to you. In an attempt to be funny, you say to her, "You have such beautiful hair; it must be a wig." Her wincing reply is yes, it is; she recently lost all her hair during surgery.

Jokes that don't work are absolutely agonizing, of course, but even these failures are considered faux pas only if they fit into one of the five faux pas categories (see page 18). In other words, the joke must be more than unsuccessful; it must also be inappropriate, embarrassing, or insulting to someone. Of course, it goes without saying that you should *never* tell jokes that are based on racial or ethnic slurs. Even jests about unusual tastes or preferences can be dangerous. A neighbor of mine once made a joke she thought was pretty safe, about some strange group of people in the South Pacific who liked to eat turkey tails. She found out the hard way that people from farms in Idaho do, too.

One of the lines below may help ease you through humor that backfires:

Recovery Lines

"I think I'll turn in my joke license."

"That's what I get for trying to be funny."

"I'm sorry, I always make bad jokes when I'm nervous. I should know better by now."

"I beg your pardon. Two years ago they replaced my funny bone and it hasn't been the same since."

"I don't even know why I told that joke. I didn't think it was funny when it was told to me. I guess I should trust my instincts from now on. Sorry you had to be part of the learning process."

..... 5 .....

PHYSICAL

FAUX PAS

■ ■ ■ ■ ■ ■ ■ ■ ■ ■ ■

SOMETIMES it's not what we say that gets us into trouble, it's what we do. A "physical faux pas" can be a misguided glance, gesture, or stare, or it can be a major mishap such as stepping on someone's foot with your spiked heel. Human beings are amazingly versatile; we can humiliate ourselves by falling down, tripping, or by dropping or spilling things; we can be caught snooping where we know we shouldn't; we can be seen straightening our panty hose in public or sticking our fingers in someone else's food. There are an infinite number of possibilities for bodily blunders.

Whatever physical faux pas may befall you, I promise that you *will* live through them. Although some of the casualties you suffer (or cause) are harder to recover from than others, there are lines, and techniques available to help you survive all but the most severe slips and stumbles.

BREAKING DRESS CODES WITH PANACHE

I don't think there are many people who have not felt that particular hot spotlight of shame that comes from being dressed incorrectly. By "incorrectly" I mean substantially different from everyone else. Except for one or two highly self-confident individuals, only a few people at the bottom of the economic scale (who may feel lucky to have clothes at all) and at the very top (who are so rich they can get away with anything) can escape the whole wrong-attire experience.

I was once invited to a ball that was to be held at a very exclusive, very private club. It was black tie, and there was to be a large dance band. When I was told by the host that there was even going to be waltzing, my decision of what to wear was solved: it would have to be my black taffeta 1940s ball gown. Now, this full-length gown is tight at the waist and then stands out full from there down, like a Scarlett O'Hara dress. It is strapless and has a red velvet, heart-shaped bodice; it's the kind of dress you automatically accessorize with long white gloves. It's so formal, it's almost theatrical. But I thought, if I am ever going to wear it, now is the time.

I don't want to prolong the agony of the memory of my entrance. Suffice to say that I arrived to find all the other women in short dresses. (This wasn't my usual crowd—how was I to know?) The host took one quick look at me, then looked away again and did not speak to me the whole evening (ahem—speaking of faux pas). In front of my own mirror at home I had felt like Cinderella going to the ball, and now I felt as if I were wearing a black pumpkin Halloween costume.

What did I do? Did I turn tail and run, go hide in the powder room, slink off to sit in the corner with my coat over my head?

Certainly not! What one must *always* do in these situations is rise to the occasion. Indeed, the more inappropriate your costume, the more you must demonstrate to the world that you are not ashamed, that you dressed that way on purpose, or that at least you are not unhappy with the way it turned out. Feign confidence: smile wider than usual, laugh more, try to exude a done-it-all, seen-it-all air of wisdom. Remember that image is an illusory thing. To a great extent, if you act as if there is nothing wrong, people will not look at you amiss. On the ball-gown evening I have described, I merely took a deep breath and adopted the attitude that it was everyone *else* who was dressed incorrectly. (Ah me, I guess the poor dears don't own ball gowns.) I waltzed, I flirted, I drank champagne. In short, I had a marvelous time.

Of course, if your outfit is inordinately unsuitable (you've worn shorts to an award ceremony, for example), you might want to arm yourself with an entertaining or interesting story about your mode of dress, before you begin to interact. "The airline lost my luggage and all my credit cards" is one way to go, although I prefer something a little bolder, such as "I've just come from meeting Donald Trump." The truth is, the wilder the lie, the more believable it is.

There are many alibis available to you for explaining your unconventional or unique accoutrements. Here are some from which to choose:

Ten Tall Tales to Explain the Way You're Dressed
1. You are going somewhere immediately afterward.
2. You have been somewhere immediately beforehand.
3. You just came from work and didn't have time to change.
4. You are winning a bet or taking a dare.
5. You never received the invitation.
6. A friend played a practical joke on you and told you this was how everyone was going to be dressed.
7. You are conducting a social science experiment for a magazine article you are writing.
8. You always dress unconventionally because it gets people's attention.
9. You never wear anything else because you believe having to pick out different clothes to wear every day enslaves you.
10. You are having a nervous breakdown.

Of course, I don't want anyone to get the idea that lying is the *only* way to go in these situations (although I often find mendacity fun, fast, and fruitful). Sometimes you may feel that it is more appropriate for you, and more effective given the circumstances, to *dwell* on your fashion faux pas instead of denying it.

Last year I was invited to just the kind of thing I usually

never go to: a bachelorette party. The women having it were all strangers to me, but Cathy, the bride-to-be, was an old friend; so I told the woman who was organizing it that I would come. "Great," she said, and then added, "Oh, and the theme is 'Tacky Cat.'"

I pondered over this theme. It sounded a little strange to me, but Cathy and I had certainly gone to many "tacky parties" in our youth, dressed in Day-Glo polyester and plastic jewelry. And so, even though the party was at a fairly expensive restaurant, I threw myself into the spirit of things and swathed myself in pink and white striped leggings, an oversized T-shirt with a rhinestone cat on it, and completed the look with whiskers applied with an eyeliner pencil.

The cab driver looked at me funny. Even in New York, people stare at you if you have whiskers on, and I found myself wishing I were already at the restaurant. I began to hope that they had booked a private room. Finally I got there, was shown to a table, and—surprise: everyone was dressed normally! Not just normally, but very conservatively—suits and sweaters and little gold earrings. Everyone gaped at me and started to giggle. Cathy hadn't arrived, and so, red-faced, I introduced myself around the table. "Love your outfit," a few of the women said. I began to think it had all been one big practical joke on me. Soon the whole restaurant was staring. (Of course, there was no private room.) It wasn't until Cathy arrived—as in the dark as I was about why I was dressed up as a cat—and began to open her presents (I hadn't even brought one, speaking of faux pas) that I realized it was *the gifts* that were supposed to follow the "tacky cat" theme.

Once I figured out what had happened, my way was clear.

When the time came for me to give Cathy her present, I stood up and whipped out my eyebrow pencil. "I am your bachelorette party kitten," I sort of meowed, "and since this is your last night to *howl*, I'm here to give you some whiskers!" Everyone cheered, and I proceeded to draw cat whiskers on Cathy as well as on the other women. (P.S.: The party got pretty wild after that. Something happens to people when you give them animal faces.)

Of course, this is admittedly an extreme example of this recovery tactic. However, as silly as this particular evening's behavior might sound, the point is that rather than apologize or try to excuse away my getup, I focused on it, exaggerated it, and made it part of the festivities. It may take a little creativity on your part, but when you can manage to turn your clothing faux pas into a weapon for social success, you can end up feeling totally victorious—having won the battle against all odds.

TOO MUCH TOUCH: HOW FAMILIARITY REALLY DOES BREED CONTEMPT

Each of us has done it to others; and all of us have had it done to us. Though the action was inadvertent and unexpected, you may suddenly realize that you have somehow crossed over that line of acceptable physical behavior and touched someone how or where you shouldn't.

More than most other faux pas, those involving touching someone in an inappropriate and/or overly familiar way are extremely subjective. Some people feel that putting your arm around someone while you're talking to them is a permissible expression of camaraderie; others feel it is an affront—even an attack. So when it comes to touch, how much is too much?

There are no strict rules in this area, but certain types of social touching (hugging, shaking hands, cheek kissing) are generally more allowed than others (pinching, slapping, poking). But no matter what kind of touching you are doing, try to make sure the person you are touching is comfortable with it. If, during a long talk with someone at a party, you occasionally lean forward and touch that person's arm to emphasize something, it's probably okay. But always be cognizant of the other person's reactions; if, every time you put that hand out, you notice his eyes darting fearfully in its direction, be courteous enough to continue the conversation minus the arm grabbing. (WARNING: If you've had too much to drink, you are a faux pas waiting to happen! Cut way down on your touching—if you can remember to—when under the influence).

In general, the following forms of touching are considered inappropriate if done by one adult to another in a social or public setting—unless they are very good friends or romantically involved (and even then some of these are iffy):

Kissing hello on the lips
Kissing on the back of the neck
Head patting
Hair ruffling
Hair stroking
Pinching
Poking
Grabbing (anywhere except the arm, and then only to stop you from running into something)
Biting, licking, nibbling, etc.
Nose tweaking

Ear pulling

Knee squeezing

Slapping (except for lightly on the back)

Not surprisingly, the perpetrators of touch faux pas are usually not aware they are committing them. They are either socially clueless or intoxicated, or they are wolves (male or female), sexual harassers, senile, psychotic, or from a culture where such behavior is acceptable. However, on a rare occasion, the victim of Too Much Touch will enlighten the person who is touching him, by saying something like, "Take your hands off me!" or "Can you please not do that to my nose?" If this should happen to you, for heaven's sake, stop whatever it is you are doing and apologize at once.

Frankly, it is not easy to regain the respect of a person whom you have offended in this manner. If possible, and if the object of your faux pas seems willing, use your physical foible to lead you both into a discussion of personal-space boundaries and why some people tend to overstep them. It will show that your regrets are sincere, and besides, you might learn something valuable about your own pawing, petting, or poking proclivities.

SPILLS, TRIPS, JOSTLES, AND BUMPS

We live in an imperfect world. Accidents happen. People get bumped into, glasses get knocked over, coffee gets sloshed on Oriental rugs, and anyone can trip over a bad spot in the floor. So when is an act of clumsiness considered a faux pas? Why are some cocktail-party collisions so embarrassing, and why is some spilled milk something you really do want to cry over?

The difference between an innocent mishap and one that classifies as a faux pas is subtle and has a lot to do with whether or not you could have avoided the incident.

For instance, let's say you have been invited to the home of a woman whom, for one reason or another, you would like to impress. Upon arriving, you enter the kitchen to ask your hostess if you can help.

"Sure," she says, indicating two large trays of food, "you can take those into the living room—but take them one at a time; they're heavy." Ever the macho man, you grab them both, throwing the woman a casual "I can manage" over your shoulder as you head gallantly to the living room. When you lose your balance and one of the trays (the one with the dip, naturally) lands upside down on the floor, you realize belatedly that you *couldn't* manage, and that it was stupid to have tried.

What makes this a faux pas is not that you attempted to carry more than you could handle, but that *you were warned.* In other words, this was an accident that could have easily been averted, a disaster caused by your own impaired judgment. Carelessness due to impaired judgment—whether it is fed by nervousness, self-consciousness, conceit, alcohol, fatigue, or deep-seated insecurity—is the essence of these types of physical faux pas. While it might not be a faux pas if a guest knocks over a glass of red wine onto her host's antique lace tablecloth, it *is* a faux pas if the reason she knocked it over is that she'd had one too many.

This may sound like overanalysis, but remember: No one goes through this thought process at the time of the faux pas. People usually just know when it is a faux pas and when it isn't. For instance, falling over into the punch bowl is always going to be seen as a faux pas (unless someone pushed you, of course), based on the assumption that if all your faculties were intact, you simply could not do such a thing. And when a certain acquaintance of mine—who shall remain nameless— tripped a blind man on the street (she wasn't watching where she was going and his cane got tangled in her stiletto heels), she knew right away that it never should have happened, and it wouldn't have if she hadn't been inordinately distracted.

These spills, trips, jostles, and bumps can take place anywhere: at a party, at the office, in a store, on the street, at the post office, at the hairdresser, in the bank, at the theater, or in church; and they can result in just looking silly or causing someone physical injury. Here is just a partial list of the embarrassing possibilities for you to try to avoid.

- spilling or dropping food or drink—on yourself, on some-one else, or on the furniture
- spilling items out of your purse, pockets, or briefcase
- dropping messy knives, forks, or spoons
- knocking over drinks, knickknacks, or lamps by gesticulating
- knocking things over with your backpack or big purse
- bumping into walls, people, or furniture
- pushing other people into walls, people, or furniture
- stepping on toes, toys, small pets, or crawling children
- jostling people who are carrying food or drink, especially *hot* food or drink
- jostling people while they are writing, taking a photo, or using a sharp object
- tripping over carpets, your own feet, or other people's feet
- tripping over babies and baby carriages while the baby is asleep

Recovery

Because of its slapstick nature, this kind of physical faux pas is often witnessed by a roomful of people. This can create a high degree of embarrassment on the part of the faux pas maker, and can make recovery very challenging ("challenging" being the modern term for "hard as hell").

First, it is vital to remember that if you have spilled or tripped when it was definitely not your fault, you must project this, lest the accident be perceived by bystanders as your faux pas. In these cases your attitude and reaction should always demonstrate that it was someone else—or an act of God—that caused you to trip on that last step or to push your sister into the ice cream. But be dignified, not vicious. A simple and somewhat vague, "I'm so sorry, I must have lost my balance" is more effective than laying direct blame on someone else. Chances are, the victim and any onlookers will know exactly whose fault it was, and your graciousness at *not* naming the culprit will actually win you dozens of recovery points.

If you *are* guilty of some conspicuous act of clumsiness that is making you want to vaporize, try not to panic. For one thing, you may find that you have some unexpected help in your struggle to redeem yourself. Quite often these very public, drastic faux pas are smoothed over with the help of kindhearted faux pas-cifists—other people who step in to save the day (and your face). This is most likely to occur when you are too busy picking things up or making sure there are no broken bones. But even if there is no one around to help you, you must make an effort at some kind of recovery. This type of faux pas demands it. (NOTE: Sometimes, whether or not your physical faux pas requires a recovery attempt depends on where you are. For example, if you are on the subway at rush hour, it is one thing to trip over someone's foot; if you are at a black-tie dinner party, it's quite another.)

The only ironclad rule in recovering from spills, trips, jostles or bumps is that if the calamity involves someone else, whatever technique or line you use *must* be accompanied by an apology. While there are, of course, techniques and lines in Chapter 3 that will apply to these situations, you basically have only three options:

1. *Truth:* This is usually the most comfortable method for people who don't like a lot of fancy footwork; however, there's

honesty and then there's honesty. For instance, honesty after spilling your martini onto someone's shoe does not mean saying, "I've obviously had too much to drink, as usual, and am now at the sloppy stage," but something more along the lines of "Oh my gosh—I'm so sorry. I don't know whether the room is tilting or I am, but I guess I had better switch to water."

2. *Lying:* Always risky to try (but always rewarding when successful). Lying works better for some faux pas than for others. I wouldn't try it for the preceding martini-sloshing incident; on the other hand, if you knock into someone from behind, you can try to convince the person that someone pushed *you.* And if you've just clumsily overturned your pocketbook in the foyer—spilling out all the humiliating, highly personal, disheveled contents—you may very well get away with "Darn! I have got to get that clasp fixed!"

3. *Downshifting:* This technique is similar to the Faux Pas-moi, except that instead of completely ignoring your dastardly deed, you *downplay* it. Act *real* casual about it. Your goal should be to diminish the power of your faux pas by at least one notch. With Downshifting, you acknowledge that you have just missed your mouth completely and that, yes, cranberry juice is running down the front of your white graduation dress, but you maintain that it's just not very important. You can effect this with a line like "Well, now, that's a silly thing," or "Hmmm. Look at that." Downshifting works because frequently, right after a faux pas, people will take their cue from you. There is always a moment or two while the event is sinking in and people are trying to put a label on it in their minds. It's your job to make them think the label

reads: NO BIG DEAL. (WARNING: You cannot use this method if you have injured someone else. Once a waitress tried this on me after spilling hot soup on my lap—instead of apologizing, she just threw me a napkin. I was livid. I must admit it was a brave Downshifting attempt, though.)

If you'd prefer to use a specific, rehearsed line, here are a few I have found effective:

"I'm trying to cut down on my drinking. I figure if I spill one out of two, I'll be cutting down by half."

"Do you want to see my license and registration?"

"I hope your homeowner's policy is current."

"I'm sorry—I'm so accident-prone right now; I've got PMS." (Warning: This line will send most men running terrified from the room.)

"Sorry! There is so much bumping and shoving going on in here, it's like the subway."

OTHER BODILY BLUNDERS: FROM THE BANAL TO THE BIZARRE

Spills, trips, jostles, and bumps are by no means the only faux pas committed with actions instead of words. There are an infinite number of ways to faux-pas with a look, gesture, movement, or activity. These blunders can range from the common (but still very rude) act of yawning in someone's face when he or she is talking to you to more bizarre bits of bungling such as walking into the closet instead of out the front door.

1 1 3

The Banal

Just the other night I was at a black-tie event where I made one of the worst kinds of commonly committed physical faux pas: A woman was telling me something about someone else at the party, and I turned around to see to whom she was referring—and actually pointed at the man!

"Jeanne!" my conversational partner reprimanded me in horror. "Aren't you supposed to be writing a *book* on faux pas?" She raised an eyebrow, as if to say, "What the heck kind of an expert are you anyway?" I was so mortified that all I could manage in response was, "You've heard of the blind leading the blind, haven't you?"

While naturally you will want to try to avoid the following unpleasant blunders, remember that you are only human. If you haven't already, you will without a doubt find yourself, at some time or another, in one or more of the following predicaments:

- You are seen pointing at someone.
- You are observed putting sugar into your soup, drinking from your finger bowl, buttering your hand instead of your roll, etc.
- You get caught staring at someone who is physically challenged or who has a disfigurement of some kind.
- You fall asleep somewhere you shouldn't—during a party, in a business meeting, at a lecture or conference, at an art opening, or in the birthing room when your wife is having a baby.
- You are caught in the act of snooping into someone's private papers or personal belongings (e.g., medicine cabinet, desk drawer, underwear drawer).

- Your clothing is not fastened properly and something falls off, down, or open at an inopportune and public moment.
- You have headphones on and realize you are talking way too loud, or you are singing out loud without your being aware of it, and people are looking at you funny.
- You get toilet paper stuck to the bottom of your shoe and you don't notice it until you've walked past four of your colleagues.
- A noise comes out of your mouth you didn't mean to make—a giggle at a funeral, a sob at a business meeting, a loud guffaw during a dramatic performance, or a snore at a wedding.
- You are caught picking your teeth, biting your nails, chewing your knuckles, gnawing your lip, or scratching your groin.

For most of the preceding transgressions you can use the same recovery methods you would for spilling or tripping (Truth, Lying, or Downshifting) or one of the many basic recovery techniques described in Chapter 3, or try one of these emergency lines:

"Yes, I was brought up in a barn."

"My mother always told me to try to make a big noise in the world."

"Whoops! They don't make buttons like they used to."

"You didn't see that."

"How much will it cost to keep you quiet about this?"

"My body will simply not follow my instructions today."

Please note: Unchecked sneezing without a handkerchief, coughing on someone's food, loud belching, and other involuntary bodily noises and functions, I will not elaborate on, for reasons of delicacy. Try to do these things discreetly or not at all, when out in public. If you do, and you're caught, your best post–faux pas course of action is a combination apology and excuse, such as "I do beg your pardon! I haven't been at all well lately." As for spitting in public, all people who engage in this practice should be put in jail.

The Bizarre

A woman I interviewed for this book told me an odd faux pas tale. She and her husband were coming back from an evening out with a female friend of his. The taxi was dropping the couple off first, and as the female friend was in the front of the car, the husband went around to lean in through the front window to talk to her and say good-bye. While talking to her, he was holding on to what he *thought* was her arm (under a thick winter coat), but what was, in fact, her breast. By the time he figured out that the shape and the feel of what he was clutching was not at all armlike, his hand had already been there for so long that he didn't want to let go suddenly and reveal that he was aware of his faux pas. He decided his only hope of not embarrassing himself and the woman further was to let her believe that he remained ignorant of his miscalculation. (Anyway, that's his story and he's stuck with it). He finished his good-bye as quickly as he could and released her.

I thought that was a pretty bizarre story until I heard the following amazing and sworn-to-be-true airplane story. Years ago, my friend Catherine had to take a three-hour flight for business. (It was one of her first business trips.) She had been up late the night before, and fell asleep right after the plane took off. She woke up to discover three disconcerting things: (1) She had slept through the entire flight; (2) she had slept through the entire flight with her head in the lap of the man next to her; and (3) she had drooled on his trousers.

What did she do? What did she say? What did *he* say? Absolutely nothing. Now, I won't get into what the man's motivations may or may not have been for letting a strange woman's head stay in his lap for three hours; but for Catherine—as it is for anyone who has made a physical faux pas of this magnitude—ignoring it was probably the best, if not the only, tack to take. If she hadn't been so groggy, she could have tried a wry "We've got to stop meeting like this," or "I guess I should have asked for a pillow," but when a person's humiliation is that intense, she usually loses the power to speak.

In both of the above faux pas, the perpetrators rightly judged that acting as if the incident had never happened was their best chance for survival. On the other hand, if your blunder is weird but not terribly ghastly—such as the time a doctor I know delivered a baby and minutes afterward his toothbrush accidentally dropped out of his pocket onto the bed where the exhausted woman lay—you can always opt for a humorous recovery line, like "Never too early to begin good dental care." Each unique faux pas situation requires a relevant line, of course. The trick to thinking up the right quip is not to allow your embarrassment to freeze your tongue. Remind yourself as often as possible that every person on earth has embarrassed himself, and that people are more empathetic than you may think.

Whatever original and harrowing form of physical faux pas you make, you can get through the experience by using the same methods you would for spills, trips, jostles, and bumps. But don't be afraid to be a little courageous in your recovery attempts. To depend on the Faux Pas-moi or Downshifting may be the safest avenue, but it's the sissy way out. You shouldn't be afraid to take some chances, to bring your faux pas out into the light and examine it. After all, what's the worst that can happen?

···· 6 ····

THE WORLD'S
BEST AND WORST
FAUX PAS

■ ■ ■ ■ ■ ■ ■ ■ ■ ■

COMPOUNDED PROBLEMS: THE MUFFED RECOVERY

Due to my penchant for trying to recover from every faux pas I make, I sometimes find myself in the unenviable position of having to deal with a muffed recovery situation. Indeed, the only problem with some of the recovery techniques and lines is that the more advanced or daring your recovery efforts are, the more apt you are to get yourself in deeper trouble, faux pas–wise, if your efforts fail. It's like betting double or nothing; you either win big or you lose big. Some of the stickiest faux pas situations I can remember being in have been caused by a flubbed recovery attempt.

Alarmed? Well, don't be. I firmly believe that if you don't lose your nerve, you can fight your way out of any mess you have created.

Let's take an example:

Not too long ago, a friend named Sharon set me up on a blind date. The fact that I don't go on too many blind dates, combined with the reality that blind dates are intrinsically nerve-racking, torturous ordeals, had put me in kind of an altered state. I was not at the top of my game, to say the least, and was therefore highly susceptible to faux pas.

We met for coffee and began exchanging the usual first-date questions. "So," I ventured, "Sharon tells me you're in real estate."

My date looked puzzled. "No, actually, I'm a graphic designer." Abashed at my faux pas, I thought back frantically to what Sharon had told me, and remembered that real estate was the profession of another guy she had talked about setting me up with but hadn't. I took a breath and trotted out what I thought would be a serviceable, if not clever, faux pas recovery.

"Oh, that must have been one of the dozens of other guys she set me up with!" I laughed.

To my horror, what I had meant to be a humorous recovery line fell flat on its face. "I guess so," was the date's unenthusiastic response. (I had muffed the recovery; he didn't understand that I was kidding and he was now under the impression that I went on so many dates with so many men, I couldn't keep them straight.)

It's in these bleak moments that you may feel like giving up. But when you have botched your recovery like this, you are in too deep to let it go. You *must* keep swimming until you reach shore. I took another breath.

"I'm sorry—that was a pathetic attempt at humor," I said earnestly. "The truth is, I'm a little nervous. I don't usually go out on blind dates. In fact, Sharon has set me up with no other guys and I have no idea where I came up with the notion of your being in real estate." I smiled and continued, "Maybe you bought and sold castles in a past life."

This may not have been a brilliant comeback, but it did smooth over the rift in the flow of things pretty well. My date loosened up after that and we had a fairly nice time, as these things go.

The secret to recovering successfully from a muffed recovery is that you must either do a total about-face as I did (recovery line #1 was a flippant remark; so recovery line #2 was a sincere confession that counteracted line #1) OR go forward strongly in the same direction. If I had wanted to use the latter version of this method, I might have tried something like "In fact, wait a minute . . . *you're* not wearing a red carnation; I think I'm supposed to be at the next table" for line #2. In other words, I could have extended the joke I had begun, so that the date would finally understand I had been kidding. In this case, because the man obviously didn't get my sense of humor, it was better to go with the about-face version of this recovery.

Not until the very moment you find yourself staring into the black hole of a flubbed faux pas recovery will you be able to decide in which direction to proceed with your survival tactic. It all depends on the nature of your primary faux pas and the subsequent disaster. But whatever you do, don't stop until you have managed to pull yourself up out of the turbulent water of your compound faux pas. You'll be glad you did.

THE NIGHTMARE OF THE MULTIPLE FAUX PAS

If you thought things couldn't get worse than the muffed recovery, think again. It's rare, but when it strikes, there is nothing so horrifying, so bewildering, or so destructive as a multiple faux pas. Multiple faux pas are the ninety-mile-an-hour hurricanes of social interaction.

The best illustration I can think of for this particular faux pas hybrid is a phone conversation that took place between two men, Doug and Randy. The reason for the call was that Randy had heard through a mutual friend (Jack) that Doug had a computer he wanted to sell, and Randy was interested. As I understand it, the conversation went something like this:

(Ring)

DOUG: Hello?

RANDY: Hi. Is this "Little Dougie"?

DOUG: (pause) Who *is* this?

RANDY: Oh, sorry, I guess not too many people besides Jack call you that . . . Uh, this is a friend of Jack's.

DOUG: Oh. Yes?

RANDY: Yeah, my name is Randy and Jack said you had a computer you were selling? He said you had to sell it because you lost your job and you, well, you know, you were about to go under and all . . . I mean . . . that is . . . I'm sure it's not that bad, but . . . well . . . so what kind of computer is it, anyway?

DOUG: It's a 386 PC, with a twelve-inch black-and-white monitor and an HP Desk Jet printer.

RANDY: You're kidding! God, what I have *now* is better than *that!* (silence) What I meant to say was, I'm looking for something a little more advanced.

DOUG: Hey—sorry I couldn't help you out, man.

RANDY: Oh no, that's all right. I'm sorry. Listen, though, if I hear of anyone who is looking for a starter system . . . that is, maybe a student or something . . .

DOUG: Look, don't worry about it.

RANDY: (pause) I guess I just better hang up now.

DOUG: I think that's a good idea.

(click)

In this one short conversation, Randy managed to commit four separate faux pas (although the last one was almost identical to the one before it). There was no recovery attempt, muffed or not, just one faux pas after another. (Randy had to lie down on the couch for an hour after the call was over.)

The above catastrophic conversation was a type-A multiple faux pas: a series of two or more *verbal* faux pas. It is also possible to commit a type-B multiple faux pas—a combination of verbal and physical faux pas—or a type-C multiple faux pas—a series of two or more physical faux pas. Here are two quick examples:

TYPE B: Joe, who is very nervous about meeting his new boss (Ms. Smith), temporarily forgets the name of his own wife when trying to introduce her to Ms. Smith. His nervousness increases, and he backs into a lamp, knocking it onto the slate floor where it smashes into a thousand pieces.

TYPE C: Overtired and stressed from too many hours at the office, Jane attends a dinner party where she has two glasses of wine and starts laughing so hard she can't stop. Out of control, she spills a glass of red wine on her blouse. She goes into the kitchen with her hostess to try to get the stain out, and, having followed behind her hostess too closely, smashes into her, sending her sprawling on the floor.

There's not much you can do to recover completely from most multiple faux pas. Here are some lines, however, to help you partially recover. (In addition, please review the EXITS on page 64. You may just want to get the hell out of there.)

Semirecovery Lines

"Somebody call an ambulance. I need oxygen or a full-body transplant or something."

"This has just become the worst day of my life."

"Hold on . . . I think my head's about to spin around."

"I think we're just both [all] having a really bad dream."

(One last note on this subject: There are a few unfortunates in the world who are so faux pas–prone that they make multiple faux pas all the time. These people have what is known as MFP Syndrome. Top research scientists in the country are currently looking for a cure.)

RACIAL FAUX PAS AND POLITICAL INCORRECTIONS

It's difficult even to discuss racial faux pas because of the profound sense of fear and shame attached to the genre. These missteps often go beyond tactlessness and reveal all too much about our subconscious attachment to stereotypes. Racial faux pas can make your stomach lurch just to hear about them, much less commit them. Unthinkingly calling a Native American an Indian giver, referring to an Asian person as "an enigmatic Oriental," or assuming a black man is the supervisor's assistant instead of the supervisor can make you want to kill yourself. Your deep sense of mortification comes from the knowledge that no matter how innocent they seem on the surface, these faux pas reveal something sinister and destructive: prejudice.

All human beings have prejudices of one kind or another. However, when I talk about racial *faux pas* I am not talking about blatant hostility or belligerence but about something more accidental. There is also a difference between faux pas and bad taste; if you tell a lot of ethnic jokes, you are probably someone who doesn't care whom he offends.

The majority of us are petrified of making one of these grievous gaffes, and it is this fear, of course, that often makes them happen. The more afraid you are of saying the wrong thing, the more certain it is that you will do just that. Most racial faux pas and politically incorrect remarks fall into faux pas category five: saying something that shows your ignorance.

If you are caught making one of these painfully embarrassing slips, try to remember the following:

Apologize without Beating Yourself Up

If you are immediately aware you have made a racial faux pas, the bravest thing (and often the best thing) you can do is to apologize sincerely to the injured party. (And in these situations you should always apologize, if at all possible, *without* using humor.) You may think that ignoring the whole thing might be better than dwelling on it; but this kind of faux pas is often so hurtful that you just have to take your medicine by letting the other person—and those within earshot—know that you understand you were in the wrong. Depending on the level of your offense, you can either not make a big deal about it—and move on to something else quickly—or you can let the person know that you are not only regretful but also trying to change.

Do not grovel, however. The deed is done. Guilt only produces more fear. The only thing expected of you is that you try to learn from your mistakes and not let the same thing happen again. Unless you have been really vicious or intentionally insulting, the other person should be able to forgive your gaffe.

Never Be Defensive

Occasionally someone will accuse you of making a racial faux pas or slur of which you do not think you are guilty. You may be in the right, but do not allow yourself to get into an argument about it. You could also be wrong. Let the person know he has given you something to think about. (And then *do* think about it.)

As for other types of politically incorrect behavior, it's virtually impossible to keep up with what's considered politically correct; furthermore, the definition of political correctness very much depends on where you are. Try to keep Anti–Faux Pas rule number two in your mind at all times: Before you speak, think about your audience. If you are talking to someone you know is an animal rights activist, don't tell her how much you enjoyed your recent quail hunt—unless your goal is controversy. But in the final analysis, all of us have to forgive each other for a lot of the prejudices and stereotypes that have been put in our heads—as long as we are making some effort to improve.

On the other hand, I think we've become a bit hypersensitive in some of these areas. The other day I ordered black coffee and was told rather curtly that the currently acceptable term was "coffee straight." I was suddenly stricken by the paranoid thought that if I went the next day to another server and asked for "coffee straight," the man would look at me furiously and mutter, "Fascist heterosexual!"

BEYOND FAUX PAS: UNSALVAGEABLE SITUATIONS

Some social scenarios or twists of fate are so outlandish, so humiliating, so harmful, or so soul-wrenching that they can no longer be classified as faux pas. While I hope none of these catastrophes will ever happen to you, it may be reassuring for you to know where the outer reaches of the faux pas universe are. No matter what kind of a fool you make of yourself tomorrow, it is not likely that you will ever do anything half so bad as what is described in these totally unsalvageable situations. In effect, examples of the extremes of embarrassment serve as an analgesic to our faux pas–related pain; they remind us that the things *we've* done that make us cringe are not so bad after all.

Performance Disasters

It's one thing to forget the name of your boss at a cocktail party, it's another to forget your lines while you are onstage or to freeze up during an important sales presentation. Sally Field once described her worst acting experience. When she was young and inexperienced, she was called upon to cry during a particular scene in a movie. At the filming there were hundreds of extras and technicians, and when the time came for her to cry, all eyes were upon her. For some reason, the tears would not come. They had to shoot the entire scene over, and when the crying cue came, again there were no tears. To this day, Ms. Field lives in terror of this moment, and of the possibility of it somehow recurring.

This is every actor's and presenter's worst nightmare. While the public humiliation factor is the same here as it is for many faux pas, this is just about the most amount of public humiliation you can have and still physically live through it.

Getting Caught Cheating

If you get caught cheating at a crossword puzzle, it may be a faux pas, but there is no recovering if you are caught cheating at poker or copying answers off someone else's test. Cheating is not a faux pas, it is a violation of society's moral code. It's also very bad for your karma. If you are caught cheating, you might want to get some spiritual help. Also, in spite of the fact that the term *faux pas* once referred to a woman's "lapse in virtue," getting caught cheating on your spouse is also not a matter for the faux pas gods, but something for you and your mate to deal with.

Geriatric-Related Incidents

A man I met told me a very strange story about his grandmother. Somehow she got confused about the difference between stockings and panty hose (or she had forgotten altogether about the invention of panty hose). In any case, one day she showed up in church wearing two new pairs of panty hose, with an extra leg hanging from each of her own legs.

I know of another elderly woman who feeds real food to a stuffed dog. The mistakes of the aged are sometimes amusing and sometimes sad, but they must always be excused. They are never considered faux pas.

Serious Damages

If your clumsiness results in real damage, it obviously does not count as a faux pas. If you cause serious physical injury, if you get someone fired, even if you spill Madeira all over a very valuable first edition of Steinbeck's *Grapes of Wrath*, none of the faux pas recovery techniques and rules in this book apply. What you *do* need is a lawyer, insurance, and maybe a new friend or two.

Ultimate Faux Pas

Every once in a while I hear a faux pas story that is so horrible, it makes anyone who hears it scream out loud. I call these gems "ultimate faux pas" because the people featured in them have reached the pinnacle of the faux pas mountain. There is no recovering from these monster faux pas; they merely make great stories.

The infamous four-person pileup happened in a French bakery in Greenwich Village. It was Saturday and the shop was crowded. A large woman had just picked up and was about to pay for a three-layer German chocolate cake, when someone near the door called her name. Whoever it was who called her caused her to become suddenly flustered (an ex-boyfriend? a Weight Watchers counselor?), and in abruptly turning away from the counter, the woman failed to notice a large purse sitting on the floor. She tripped, and her arms and the cake flew into the air. She fell into a man waiting in line, who knocked into the person behind him and so on, just like dominoes. In the end, four people and the remains of a chocolate cake lay sprawled on the floor.

I heard another story about a situation so bizarre and so awful that I had trouble believing it was true, though the narrator of the tale swore that it was.

After many months, a lovesick guy (I'll call him John) finally got up the nerve to ask out the object of his affections (I'll call her Ellie). John was extremely anxious about this date and felt a real need to impress her. The trouble started when at the very beginning of this date—which was to include a train trip to Long Island—John split his pants all the way up the back. In trying to hide this fact from Ellie, he made up an excuse to stop on the way to the train station at a clothing store, where he ran in and bought another pair of pants, while the oblivious Ellie was off buying spring water or something. John figured he'd change on the train, and that Ellie would be none the wiser. As soon as they were on the train, before they were even seated, John excused himself and went off to change his pants. There was no rest room on the train, so his only option became the open area in between cars. In his hurry to make the switch, he took off his ruined pants and threw them off the train. Reaching into the store bag, he pulled out—a woman's cotton sweater! He realized that in his rush, he must have picked up the wrong bag at the store.

John wrapped the sweater around himself and thought for a few terrible minutes. He tried to imagine what he could say to Ellie to explain why he had no pants. The train was just pulling into the first station. He got off the train, took a cab home, and never saw or spoke to the woman again. (Perhaps she'll read this story and a great mystery in her life will be solved.) John must have known that under the circumstances there was no saving face; there was no recovery, there was only escape.

As drastic as these terrible tales are, the winner of the worst-faux-pas-in-the-world contest has to be George Bush, upon the unforgettable occasion, in January 1992, of the regurgitation of his dinner onto the lap of the premier of Japan. Throwing up on someone, especially a head of state, is, after all, the ultimate faux pas.

FAMOUS FAUX PAS

We all enjoy reading and hearing about celebrities and fictional characters who commit faux pas. It's comforting to us to know that someone who is at the top of his profession is still capable of embarrassing himself in public; and we love watching the protagonists in our favorite novels, movies, or TV shows committing the exact same forms of social suicide we do. But do the makers of these famous faux pas know how to survive them? Let's take a look at some well-known faux pas and see how they were handled:

Famous Faux Pas #1

In 1990, in a game against the Detroit Tigers, Steve Lyons of the Chicago White Sox slid into first and was pronounced safe. During an argument that ensued, Lyons pulled down his pants in full view of fifteen thousand people and began to brush the dirt off his legs. When the crowd cheered wildly, the embarrassed athlete quickly pulled his pants back up.

The Recovery: When asked about the incident later, Lyons said, "I just forgot where I was." This after-the-fact, rather weak excuse was not great but probably the best anyone could do under the circumstances.

Famous Faux Pas #2

In one of the most famous scenes in *Gone With the Wind,* Scarlett O'Hara pulls Ashley Wilkes into his library to confess her love to him—in a very unladylike manner. Later, after Ashley leaves and Scarlett has smashed a vase in frustration, Rhett Butler reveals himself; he had *overheard* the whole embarrassing scene. In her emotional state, Scarlett has broken one of the cardinal Anti–Faux Pas rules: *Always be sure of who is within earshot.*

The Recovery: Scarlett tries to brave it out by blaming Rhett for the faux pas ("Sir, you should have made your presence known!"). This is completely unsuccessful and only makes things worse. This is, in fact, a muffed recovery. Downshifting followed by a fast exit would have been my choice.

Famous Faux Pas #3

A few years ago, TV hosts Regis Philbin and Kathie Lee Gifford were interviewing Art Garfunkel about a book he had written. At least twice during the interview, Regis called Mr. Garfunkel "Paul" (as in Garfunkel's more famous ex-partner, Paul Simon). Kathie Lee kept yelling at Regis in that playful way she has: "Reeeg!!!"

The Recovery: Regis makes so many faux pas that they have become part of his charm. Here he used his usual recovery method, a version of the Self-Effacing Apology (see page 46), which goes something like "Jeez, I'm so sorry. I'm not getting any younger, you know . . . I'm out of *control!*" It goes well with his personality. But the fact that in this case Regis kept repeating the faux pas made a total recovery impossible.

Famous Faux Pas #4

In Jane Austen's *Pride and Prejudice,* Elizabeth Bennet is caught nosing around Pemberly, Mr. Darcy's estate, with her aunt and uncle, when Mr. Darcy comes home unexpectedly and catches them. The most embarrassing element of the situation is that Miss Bennet has only recently, but quite forcefully, turned down an offer of marriage from Mr. Darcy.

The Recovery: This is a true case of Faux Pas-cifism. Mr. Darcy successfully heals the emotional pain of the moment and restores much of Miss Bennet's equilibrium by behaving in a more gentlemanly and respectful manner toward her than he ever had before. He asks civilly after Miss Bennet's family and pays her the high compliment of asking her to meet his sister. His manner implies that her being at Pemberly is not a faux pas but is instead his good fortune. No one writes about faux pas and their recovery better than Jane Austen.

Famous Faux Pas #5

The Guinness Book of World Records lists one of the most famous faux pas as one perpetrated by a multimillionaire named James Gordon Bennett on New Year's Day in 1877. Apparently he got very inebriated, climbed in a window of his fiancée's Fifth Avenue mansion, mistook the fireplace for a plumbing fixture, and relieved himself in front of family members.

The Recovery: There was none. His engagement broken, he went off to live in Paris. This was obviously a "beyond faux pas" situation (wherein there is no recovery, only escape), although perhaps today one could have pled some sort of temporary insanity.

FAUX PAS-ITIVES: THE HAPPY-ENDING FAUX PAS

Certainly I haven't covered every faux pas ever made or every potential faux pas situation. There are millions of existing possibilities, and life's ever-changing social strata create new faux pas opportunities every day. And, as with new viruses, we have to keep coming up with new antibiotics, new versions of recovery cures.

In spite of the pain and suffering they may cause, faux pas are essential to society's well-being. Think of how boring, how lifeless, social events would be without the ever-present, just-below-the-surface possibility of a faux pas popping up at any moment. Faux pas define our boundaries, but they also break down barriers between people and melt the icy facades of society's rules; they are like messy weeds coming up through the cracks in the sidewalk. Committing faux pas keeps us humble and ensures that we continue to improve our interactions with the world, for how else do we learn but from our mistakes?

Perhaps most important, faux pas also make up many of life's most interesting, memorable occurrences. They are sometimes the only thing people will remember about an event, long after the water stains have been removed from the piano. You never know: someday, years from now, when you're traveling on some newfangled high-speed train, someone may come up to you and say, "Hey, weren't you the person who insulted Mrs. Weatherby's fruit cake?" And before you know it, the two of you will have bonded over the memory (unless, of course, the stranger turns out to be Mr. Weatherby).

Many faux pas even come with their own silver lining. These are mishaps that end up improving your life in some way. If you don't believe me, you should ask my friend Beth.

One cold and rainy night two years ago, Beth turned down a date—partially because she was in a bad mood—with a man to whom she wasn't really attracted. She told him she had the flu. She later decided to have dinner in a neighborhood restaurant with a friend. As fate would have it (as fate often does), the rejected man showed up at the very same restaurant.

Beth did not speak to him, but instead ate her meal (seasoned with guilt), and tried hard to look as if she really did have the flu. By the next day, however, her contrition had grown to such proportions that she telephoned the man, whose name is Carl, apologized profusely, and begged him to let her take him out to dinner.

Guess what? Beth and Carl have been cohabiting for almost a year now. They are very much in love, thanks to the faux pas that brought them together.

■　■　■

I hope after reading this book that you have shed some of your faux pas phobia and honed your faux pas survival skills, and that you have found the faux pas lore herein helpful and fun. Never forget that whatever faux pas come your way, you can and will survive them. (Don't be surprised if you eventually even learn to relish the memory of some of them.) Also consider this: Faux pas are not an entirely negative phenomenon. If everyone were continually making faux pas, it might do the world some good. Letting our guard down in dealing with each other, ignoring social conventions, and refusing to be embarrassed by our foibles could help to raise the level of consciousness of the whole human species.

On the other hand, nobody really wants to be the person at the black-tie party who sits on the Boston cream pie.

INDEX

host faux pas, 78–79
  recovery lines, 78–79
humor
  as defense, 53
  as faux pas, 98–99
  recovery lines, 99
  sample lines, 53–54
Humphry, Mrs., 17

I

ignorance, admitting, 26
ignoring as denial, 57–58
impressions, 37
inappropriate behavior, 19

J

jostles, 108–13
  recovery, 110–13
  recovery lines, 113

K

kidding as denial, 57
kissing as physical faux pas, 105
knee squeezing as physical faux pas, 106

L

letter writing as a response, 69
lines

excuse, 51–52
humor, 53–54
lines (recovery)
  appearance faux pas, 77
  bad language and breaking taboos, 87
  child's faux pas, 98
  death, faux pas concerning, 96–97
  departure mistakes, 76
  emergency, 115–16
  gift faux pas, 82–83
  greeting goofs, 75
  guest faux pas, 79–80
  health and hospital horrors, 91
  host faux pas, 78–79
  humor faux pas, 98–99
  office offenses, 88
  restaurant and food, 90
  semirecovery lines, 124
  sexual faux pas, 84–85
  spills, trips, jostles, and bumps, 113
  telephone faux pas, 93
  written faux pas, 95
loudmouth syndrome, 34–37
Lyons, Steve, 131–32

M

missed connections, 37–38
misunderstanding as denial, 55–56